THE ENGLISH YOU NEED FOR THE OFFICE

A PICTURE PROCESS VOCABULARY

Susan Dean and Lawrence J. Zwier

Asia-Pacific Press Holdings

Asia-Pacific Press Holdings Ltd
22nd Floor, Lane Crawford House
70 Queen's Road Central, Hong Kong
Tel: (852) 520-1205 / 810-8728
Fax: (852) 521-5700 / 865-0521

The English You Need for the Office
A Picture Process Vocabulary

Susan Dean & Lawrence J. Zwier

10 9 8 7 6 5 4 3 2 1
06 05 04 03

ISBN 962 328 019 X

Illustrations: K.B. Jang
Design: Compass

Printed by Daero Co., Korea

Contents

SECTION V: USING TELEPHONES AND FAXES

SECTION VI: USING COMPUTERS AND OTHER OFFICE MACHINES

SECTION VII: MONEY MATTERS

SECTION VIII: MAINTAINING THE OFFICE

APPENDICES

To the Student

The English You Need for the Office (EYNO) introduces vocabulary for talking about daily processes in an office. *EYNO* highlights verbs—words for doing or acting. With a larger vocabulary of verbs, you can more clearly speak or write about what happens in your life. The pictures make it easy for you to see what the new vocabulary means. To learn the spoken forms of key vocabulary, listen to the recorded version of this book. At the back of the book is Conversation Practice Material Chapter by Chapter to help students with natural dialogues. These are also available in recorded form.

Organization

Each chapter of this book is about a process. The chapters are grouped into eight larger sections, according to some aspect of working in an office. You may use the chapters in any order you like. For example, you can go from Chapter 10 to Chapter 33 and then Chapter 7 if you like.

Each chapter has a list of "key vocabulary"—the most important words and phrases from the chapter. The meanings of the key vocabulary are shown in the pictures. Each chapter also has a "For Special Attention" section to explain some key vocabulary more fully.

A milti-skills activity book is available separately.

How to Use *The English You Need for the Office*

This book can be used in a class or by yourself at home. If you are studying by yourself, think about what you did at work—sending E-mail, attending meetings, making a report, etc. How could you describe it in English? Find the process in this book and study the pictures and words together. Use the pictures to help you remember what you do as you take part in one of the pictured actions.

The index is one of your best tools for learning new vocabulary. If you learn a new word in one context, look it up in the index and notice the other pages it appears on.

If you have an idea, but you don't know the words for it: (1) go to the table of contents; (2) look for an activity related to your idea; (3) go to the chapter and look at the pictures; (4) read the English related to the pictures. If you can't find the right process in the table of contents, flip through the pages until you see some pictures about your idea.

Other Hints

- After you have found a word you are interested in, read the entire chapter where you found it. Your word may appear more than once in the chapter.
- Notice how the word fits into sentences. Learning a vocabulary item means learning how it works with other words.
- Think about differences between how you do an activity and how it is described in the book. No two people's lives are exactly the same. Try using your new vocabulary to describe the activity your way, instead of the way it is in the book. This is an excellent way to make this new vocabulary your own.

1

Getting Ready for Work

Key Vocabulary

VERBS

brush	put [put]
buy [bought]	put on
check	read
drive [drove]	shut
drop off	take [took] a
eat [ate]	shower
get [got] dressed	wake [woke]
get ready	up
grab	watch
iron	wear [wore]
leave [left]	
make [made]	
pack	
pick out	

NOUNS

alarm clock	jacket
bag	khaki pants
blouse	laundry
breakfast	loafers
briefcase	lunch
brown bag	milk
bus schedule	morning
bus stop	muffin
cereal	news
clock	newspaper
closet	pants
clothes	panty hose
coffee	paper
coffee maker	polo shirt
door	skirt
dress	sweater
dress shirt	teeth
dress shoes	tie
dry cleaner	time
house	work
iron	
ironing board	

OTHERS

casual (adj.)
on the way (adverbial)
ready (adj.)

выбрала

closet

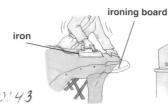

iron   ironing board

0:43

0:37

Tina picked out some clothes to wear.

While she ironed her blouse...

...she watched the morning news.

clock
milk
coffee maker
cereal

0:47

Then she got dressed.

As she made breakfast, she checked the time.

Then she ate breakfast and read the newspaper.

B 7

brown bag

After breakfast, Tina brushed her teeth.

Then she packed a lunch...

...and put some papers in her briefcase.

For Special Attention

- When you **check the time**, you look at the clock quickly to see what time it is.
- If you **pack a lunch**, you put it in a bag or lunch box and take it to work to eat.
- A **dry cleaner** cleans clothing that can't be washed in a washing machine.
- When you **grab** something, you take hold of it quickly.

- When Matt **checked** his bus **schedule**, he looked quickly at it to see when the bus would come.
- **On the way** to the bus stop means "while going to the bus stop."
- **Dress clothes** are more formal than **casual** clothes.
- **Khaki pants** are casual pants, usually made of cotton. They are worn by both men and women.

She shut the door as she left the house.

> Hi. I have two blouses and a skirt.

> They'll be ready Friday.

laundry

She dropped off some laundry at the dry cleaners.

Then she drove to work.

alarm clock

Matt woke up...

...and took a shower.

He put his clothes on...

...and he grabbed his bag.

> It will come in ten minutes.

He checked his bus schedule.

TJS

On the way to the bus stop...

> A muffin and coffee, please.

...he bought a muffin and coffee.

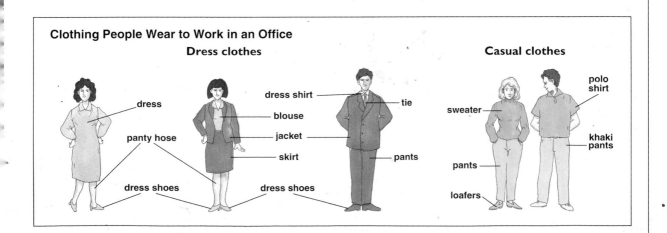

Clothing People Wear to Work in an Office

Dress clothes

dress
panty hose
dress shoes

dress shirt
blouse
jacket
skirt
dress shoes

tie
pants

Casual clothes

polo shirt
sweater
khaki pants
pants
loafers

7

2 Arriving at the Office

Key Vocabulary

VERBS
arrive
enter
go [went] into
go through
  (security)
hang [hung]
make [made]
  small talk
open
park
say [said] good
  morning

set [set]
sit [sat] down
take [took]
  (an elevator)
take out
unlock
walk
work on

NOUNS
briefcase
building
coat
coat rack
company lot
coworker
cubicle
department
desk
door
elevator
floor
guard
hall
office
paper
receptionist
security
small talk
work area

Tina parked in the company lot.

She entered the building...

> Good morning, Gladys.

> Good morning, Ms. Perez.

guard

...and said good morning to the receptionist.

After going through security (see p. 10)...

> See you later.

...she took an elevator...

...up to her floor.

For Special Attention

- Tina drives to work, so she **parks** her car.
- **company lot** = parking lot that belongs to the company
- **receptionist** = a person who makes appointments and receives clients and guests
- **to take an elevator** = to ride in it to your floor

- **a floor** = one level of a building
- **coworkers** = people you work with. Another word for them is *colleagues*.
- **Small talk** is very light conversation–about the weather, sports, etc.
- **down the hall** = along a hallway

- Tina **hangs** her coat on a coat rack.
  Other places to hang coats:

  on a hook **in a closet**

  on a hanger

She went into her department's work area.

She said good morning to some of her coworkers...

...and made some small talk.

She walked down the hall to her office.

She unlocked the door.

She hung her coat on the coat rack.

She set her briefcase on her desk.

She sat down at her desk.

She opened her briefcase and took out some papers to work on.

3 Going through Security

ограничиваю

Security systems guard restricted areas—places open to only a few people.

Key Vocabulary

VERBS

ask	open
call up	put [put]
check	recognize
come [came]	return
enter	say [said] good
forget [forgot]	morning
give [gave]	stop
go [went] in	think [thought]
go through	unlock
guard	wave (someone)
identify	through
let [let]	work

NOUNS

access code	key card
badge	machine
card	pass
desk	restricted area
door	security
guard	security system
guard post	slot
guard shack	supervisor
guardhouse	

ADJECTIVES

electronic
temporary

For Special Attention

- **Electronic systems** use machines to identify people.
- **Access code** = a number that lets you get in. Some systems use **passwords** (made of letters) instead of code numbers.
- You wear a **badge**. It tells who you are, so it is one kind of I.D. (identification).
- When you **recognize** someone, you remember seeing him/her before.
- A **pass** is a piece of paper that lets you get into a place.
- **temporary** = for only a short time

With an Electronic System

Alice put her key card into the slot in the security system.

Then she entered her access code.

The machine returned her card...

...and the door unlocked.

With a Guard (1)

Tina said good morning to the guards at the security desk.

They checked her badge.

One guard waved her through...

...while the other opened the door.

With a Guard (2)

Matt forgot his badge,...

...so the guards stopped him.

He thought they might recognize him,...

...but they didn't.

They asked him where he worked.

They called up a supervisor,...

...who came to the desk and identified him.

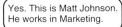

The guard gave him a temporary pass...

...and let him go in.

Guards can be found:

indoors

at desks

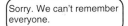
at guard posts

and

outdoors

at guardhouses or guard shacks
(one kind of guard post)

11

Key Vocabulary

VERBS

arrive
be [was] in
check
find [found]
move
open
print
punch in

put [put]
put back
report
show
sign in
write [wrote]

NOUNS

board
card
clock
column
date
in/out board
marker
name
page
rack
sign-in book
slot
system
time
time card
time clock
today
work
worker

OTHERS

else (adv.)
magnetic (adj.)

For Special Attention

Showing You Have Arrived

1. With an In/Out Board

NAME	IN	OUT	LUNCH
ALBERTSON, KAY		⊙	
HIROSE, MINORU		⊙	
JOHNSON, MATTHEW		⊙	
PETERS, SUSAN		⊙	
SEVILE, ANDREW	⊙		

Matt found his name on the board.

IN	OUT
	⊙
	⊙
⊙	

He moved his magnetic marker...

AME	IN	OUT
N, KAY		⊙
NORU		⊙
MATTHEW	⊙	

...to the "in" column.

NAME	IN	OUT	LUNCH
ALBERTSON, KAY		⊙	
HIROSE, MINORU		⊙	
JOHNSON, MATTHEW	⊙		
PETERS, SUSAN		⊙	
SEVILE, ANDREW	⊙		

Now, the board showed that Matt was in.

- **Magnetic things** stick to some kinds of metal. The in/out board is made of metal.
- In a chart or table there are **columns** and **rows** (or lines).
- **to check a clock** = to look quickly at it to find out the time
- If you are **in** (in the office), you are present at work.

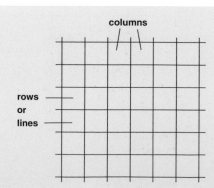

- **someone else** = a different person
- "Albert **punched in**" = Albert punched his card to show he was in.

2. With a Sign-in System

Alice opened the sign-in book...

...to the page for today's date.

She wrote her name in the "name" column.

She checked the clock...

...and wrote in the time.

Then someone else signed in.

3. With a Punch-in System

Albert took his time card from the rack.

He put it into the slot of the time clock.

The time clock punched him in...

...by printing the date and time on his card.

Albert put his card back in the rack.

Then another worker punched in.

5 Getting Settled at the Office

Key Vocabulary

VERBS

arrange	take [took]
check	take (a sip)
get [got] settled	take out
go [went]	turn on
hang [hung] up	water
look	
pour	
put [put]	
roll up	
set [set]	
sit [sat] down	

NOUNS

briefcase	refrigerator
coat	sip
coat room	sleeve
coffee	
coffee pot	
computer	
desk	
desk lamp	
diary	
frame	
hook	
jacket	
kid	
lunch	
lunch room	
mug	
office	
paper	
picture	
plants	

Matt hung his coat up in the coat room.

Then he went to his desk.

He set his briefcase on top of his desk.

Then he took his lunch to the lunch room.

For Special Attention

- A **coat room** is large enough to walk into. (A closet usually isn't.)
- A **lunch room** is a place to eat lunch, but it usually does not have a restaurant in it. A lunch room is also called a break room.
- Another word for **refrigerator** is fridge.

- Matt brought his lunch from home. This is called a **bag lunch** or a **sack lunch**. To bring a lunch from home is called "**brown bagging**."
- After you turn something on, it works or runs.
- To **arrange** things, you put them in the right places.

- **a sip** = a very small drink
- **kids** = children
- **to get settled** = get yourself organized and ready for work

He put his lunch in
the refrigerator.

coffee pot

mug

He poured himself
some coffee.

He hung his jacket
up on a hook.

He rolled up his sleeves...

...and sat down at his desk,

He turned on his computer...

...and his desk lamp.

He took some papers out of
his briefcase...

...and arranged the things
on his desk.

Other Things People Do as They Get Settled

water their plants

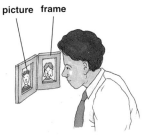

picture   frame

look at pictures of
their kids

take a sip of coffee

check their diary
(see p.16)

Key Vocabulary

VERBS

ask
call (on a phone)
cancel
check
find [found] out
have [had]
make [made] (a list)
pencil in
plan
reschedule
schedule
write [wrote] in

NOUNS

afternoon	lunch meeting
appointment	meeting
appointment	month
book	morning
button	palmtop
calendar	PDA
call	personal
conflict	computer
cradle	schedule
date	screen
date book	slot
day	software
desktop	stylus
diary	task
display	time slot
electronic	to-do list
organizer	week

ADJECTIVES

early
free

For Special Attention

Scheduling Tools

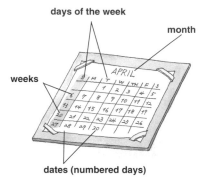

days of the week
month
weeks
dates (numbered days)

desktop calendar

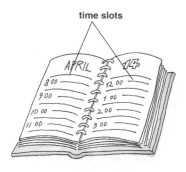

time slots

calendar / appointment book / date book / diary

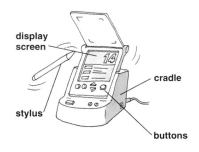

display screen
stylus
cradle
buttons

personal digital assistant (PDA) / palmtop / electronic organizer

scheduling software (on a personal computer)

- **check a calendar** = look quickly at it to find information
- **appointment** = an arrangement to meet someone at a certain time
- You make: - appointments
  - lists
  - phone calls

- In a calendar, a **slot** is a time period.
- **A free slot** = a time period with nothing scheduled. Also called an "opening."

- To **pencil** something **in** is to put it on your schedule although you may have to change it.

Planning Your Day

Tina checked her calendar.

free slots

appointment

She had appointments at 10:00 and 2:30, but she had a few free slots in the early morning and early afternoon.

She made a to-do list...

...and penciled in a few tasks.

Okay, Bob. See you at lunch.

Someone called to ask Tina for a lunch meeting,...

...so she wrote him in.

Mr. Dunyon wants a managers' meeting at 3:00.

Oh, well, I'll be there.

Then she found out that there was a meeting at 3:00.

Now she had a schedule conflict.

Annie? This is Tina Perez.

So she made a call...

I'm afraid I can't meet you at 2:30. Something has come up.

...to cancel her 2:30...

Would tomorrow afternoon be okay?

...and reschedule it.

Key Vocabulary

VERBS

blink	miss
check	pick up
delete	play
enter	press
exit	push
finish	replay
hang [hung]	save
up	write [wrote]
listen	down

NOUNS

call	phone
caller	phone line
display	phone number
information	PIN
key	pound key
message	receiver
message	star key
button	telephone
message light	time
name	voicemail
number keys	
part	

ADJECTIVES

first	next
new	

The message light on Albert's phone was blinking...

...so he pressed the message button...

...and picked up the receiver.

Then he entered his PIN.

For Special Attention

- **Phone** is a short way of saying "telephone."
- One telephone can have more than one **phone line**. Each line has a separate button.
- On most modern telephones you **dial** by pushing buttons.
- **PIN** = personal identification number
- If you **delete a message**, you remove it from your voicemail.
- When you **miss** something, you don't see or hear it.
- When you **replay** something, you listen to it again.
- When you **save a message**, you keep it on your voicemail.
- When **using voicemail**, number keys have different uses. For example, pressing one number key might save a message and pressing a different key might delete a message.
- The **star** (or asterisk) **key** and the **pound** (or hash) **key** have different uses also.
- When you **exit** voicemail, you stop using voicemail.

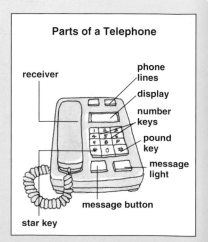

Parts of a Telephone

receiver

phone lines

display

number keys

pound key

message light

message button

star key

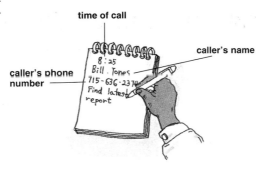

He listened to his first new message...

...and wrote down some information.

Then he pushed a key to delete the message.

While playing his next message,...

...he missed part of it.

So he replayed it.

Then he saved the message by pressing a key.

After he finished listening to all his new messages,...

...he pushed the star key to exit voicemail...

...and hung up the phone.

Taking a Coffee Break

Key Vocabulary

VERBS

be [was] up
count out
go [went] into
leave [left]
look
make [made]
make small talk
offer
open
pour
push
put [put]
read [read]
remove
return
say [said]
share
sit [sat] down
stop
take [took]
use
want

NOUNS

announcement	restroom
bag	small talk
bin	snack
break time	tea
break room	tea bag
bulletin board	vending
button	machine
change	watch
coffee	water
coffee break	work
coffee maker	
coin	
coin return	
coin slot	
company	
cookies	
cup	
money	
newspaper	
notice	

ADJECTIVE

hot

Tina and Albert went into the break room.

Tina poured a cup of coffee...

...and Albert made tea.

They sat down with Alice, who was reading the newspaper.

Albert opened a bag of cookies...

... and offered to share them with Alice and Tina.

For Special Attention

- When you **take a break**, you stop working for a short time. You can also say you **go on break**.
- When you **make small talk**, you talk about unimportant subjects, such as the weather.
- If break time **is up**, your break is finished.

- A **bulletin board** is a place to put information so it can be seen by many people.
- **Announcements, notices** and **signs** give information.
- **Change** is the money left over or returned after you buy something.

What's the forecast this weekend?

Cooler.

I hope it doesn't rain!

They made small talk.

Oh. It looks like it's time to get back.

Then Tina looked at her watch and said break time was up.

As they left the break room,...

bulletin board

announcement

notice

Let's take yoga!

...Alice and Tina stopped to look at the company bulletin board.

Albert used the restroom.

We're back.

Then they returned to work.

Using a Vending Machine

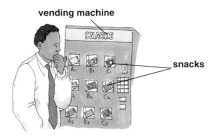

vending machine

snacks

Albert looked at the snacks in the vending machine.

25, 50, 75...

He counted out some money.

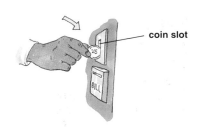

coin slot

Then he put the coins into the coin slot...

...and pushed the buttons for the snack he wanted.

coin return

He removed his change from the coin return.

bin

Then he took his snack out of the bin.

Eating Lunch in a Cafeteria

Key Vocabulary

VERBS
ask for
be [was] out of
eat [ate]
get [got]
give [gave]
go [went]
join
make [made]
order
pick up
put [put]
return
ring [rang] up
say [said]
spoon (up)
take [took]
throw [threw] away

NOUNS
beverage
bowl
cafeteria
cart
cash register
cashier
chicken
counter
dessert bar
dining area
dinner
fish
garbage
garbage can
ladle
lemonade
line
lunch
meal
menu
napkin
plate
portion

salad
salad bar
sandwich bar
server
silverware
soup
spatula
steam table
table
tongs
tray

OTHERS
clean (adj.)
instead (adv.)

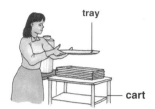

Alice took a clean tray from the cart.

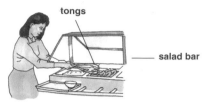

She made a salad at the salad bar.

Navy bean soup, please.

At the steam table she ordered a bowl of soup.

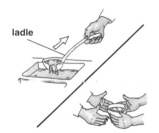

The server spooned it up and gave it to her.

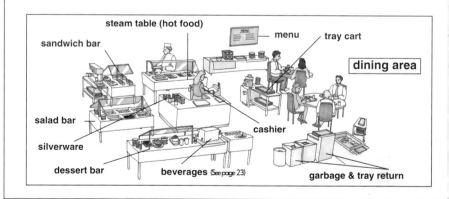

For Special Attention

- A **steam table** keeps cooked food hot in a cafeteria.
- A **server** is a cafeteria worker who may prepare and give you your food.
- When you **spoon up** food, you take it out of one container with a ladle or other large spoon and put it in another container.
- **silverware** = knives, forks, and spoons

- When you **go through** a line, you move along in a row or line.
- To **be out of** something means to not have any left.
- A **portion** is a piece, part or serving of something.
- To **ring up** means to add up the cost of everything using a cash register.
- Matt **joined** Alice by sitting at her table.

Matt went through the line behind Alice.

He ordered a chicken dinner...

He ordered a chicken dinner...

...but the server said they were out of chicken.

Matt asked for the fish instead.

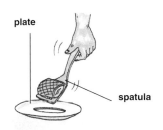

The server put a portion of fish on a plate...

...and gave it to Matt.

At the beverage counter, Matt got some lemonade.

He picked up some silverware and napkins.

Then the cashier rang up his meal.

He joined Alice at a table.

Later, they threw away their garbage...

...and returned their trays.

Eating a Bag Lunch

Key Vocabulary

VERBS
carry
close
crumple up
eat [ate]
finish
loosen
offer
pour
put [put]
remove
set [set]
sip
start
take [took]
take out
throw [threw] away
unwrap
wrap

NOUNS
bag	plastic
bag lunch	refrigerator
bite	restaurant
chips	sandwich
container	soda
cover	soup
fast food	start button
food	table
garbage	timer
leftovers	twist tie
lunch box	vacuum bottle
microwave	wrapper
milk	

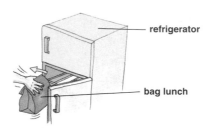

Tina removed her bag lunch from the refrigerator.

She took a plastic container of soup out of the bag...

...and loosened the cover on the container.

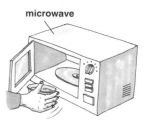

Then she put the container in the microwave,...

...set the timer...

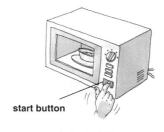

... and started the microwave.

For Special Attention

- A **bag lunch** is any kind of lunch you bring from home.
- When you **set the timer** on the microwave, it tells the microwave how long to cook your food.
- **unwrap something** = remove the covering
- **Fast food** is cooked and served quickly. If you order it "to go" you take it away from the restaurant and eat it somewhere else.
- A **vacuum bottle** keeps drinks hot or cold.
- **Twist ties** wrap around the tops of bags to keep them closed.
- When you **sip** something, you take small drinks.
- **leftovers** = food not eaten during a meal; leftovers might be saved and eaten later
- When you **crumple up** a piece of paper, you make it into a wrinkled ball.

She carried her soup to a table.

wrappers

Albert unwrapped some food from a fast-food restaurant.

Tina poured milk from her vacuum bottle.

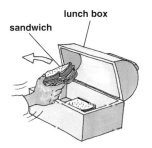

sandwich   **lunch box**

Matt took a sandwich out of his lunch box.

twist tie

Then he removed the twist tie from a bag of chips...

Would anyone like some chips?

...and offered some to Tina and Albert.

Matt took a bite of his sandwich.

Albert sipped his soda.

Tina ate her soup.

When she finished eating, she closed her container.

leftovers

Matt wrapped up his leftovers.

Albert crumpled up his wrappers.

garbage

Then they threw away their garbage.

25

Key Vocabulary

VERBS

change
deposit
eat [ate]
eat out
finish
get [got]
  some sun
give [gave]
go [went]
go swimming
have [had]
mail
make [made]
order
pay [paid]
pick out
play
put [put] on
read [read]
run [ran] errands
sit [sat]
spend [spent]

take [took]
  (a shower)
take (a walk)
talk
use
walk
work out

NOUNS

activity
ashtray
bank
bill
birthday card
card
cigarette
clothes
coworker
errand
exercise
  equipment
gym shorts
health club
locker
locker room
lunch
lunch special
lunchtime
money

package
park
park bench
paycheck
phone call
pool
post office
restaurant
sneakers
tip
T-shirt
walk
weights

OTHERS

personal (adj.)
outdoors (adv.)

Eating Out

Alice and her coworkers went to a restaurant.

She ordered the lunch special.

They talked and ate lunch.

After lunch, they all gave money to pay the bill and tip.

Working Out

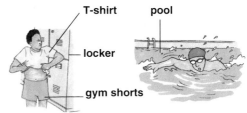

Albert and Matt went to the health club.

Albert changed clothes in the locker room.

Matt went swimming,...

...and Albert used the exercise equipment.

When he finished, Albert took a shower.

Running Errands

The postage will be two dollars.

mailing a package at the post office

I'd like to put this in my savings.

depositing a paycheck at the bank

This one looks good!

picking out a birthday card

Taking a Walk / Going Outdoors

putting on sneakers

walking in a park

sitting on a park bench

getting some sun

For Special Attention

- A **lunch special** is a meal sold at a cheaper price at lunchtime.
- A **bill** is the amount of money owed. The **tip** is extra money given to a waiter for good service.
- A **health club** is a place where people exercise.
- You **run errands** when you go on short trips to do small, necessary tasks.
- **Sneakers** are shoes used for sports. They have rubber bottoms.
- A **personal phone call** is not related to your job, e.g., making an appointment for a haircut or calling a friend.
- A **smoking area** is a special place in or outside a building where people may smoke.

Other Lunchtime Activities

reading

cards

playing cards

I'd like to make an appointment for a haircut, please.

making a personal phone call

ashtray

SMOKING AREA

having a cigarette

Ending the Workday

Key Vocabulary

VERBS

call
cross off
do [did]
eat [ate]
end
go [went]
have [had]
have to
leave [left]
lock
look
meet [met]
print
put [put]
put on

return
rinse out
say [said]
say goodbye
shut [shut] off
sign out
straighten
turn off
type
unplug
work

NOUNS

briefcase
coffee maker
computer
courier
coworker
cup
deadline
desk
drawer
file
filing cabinet
home
husband
item

jacket
key
light
list
lock
office
page
paper
power switch
printer
snack
thing
time
workday

ADJECTIVE

late

It was almost time to go home.

list

Matt looked at his list of things to do...

... and crossed some items off.

He straightened some things on his desk...

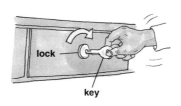

lock

key

...and locked his desk drawer.

filing cabinet

file

Then he returned a file to the filing cabinet. (See p. 48.)

For Special Attention

- A list of things to do is often called a **"to-do list."** As you do the things on the list, you **cross** them **off**, or draw a line through them.
- When you **straighten** things on your desk, you make your desktop neater.

- When you **rinse** something **out**, you run water into it to clean it.
- When you **shut off** something, you turn it off.
- A **deadline** is a day or time by which something must be done.

When you "meet a deadline," you finish the work on time – when it is supposed to be done.

- A **courier** delivers letters and packages. (See page 56.)

coffee maker

He rinsed out his cup and unplugged the coffee maker.

Then he put some papers in his briefcase...

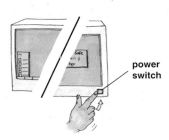

power switch

...and shut off his computer. (See p. 71.)

He put on his jacket,...

Bye, Tina.

See you tomorrow, Matt.

...said goodbye to a coworker...

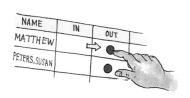

NAME	IN	OUT
MATTHEW		
PETERS, SUSAN		

...and signed out before leaving. (See p. 30.)

Working Late: Tina had a deadline to meet so she had to work late.

I've got something that has to be sent today.

Tina called her husband and said she would be late.

She typed at the computer. (See p. 72.)

She ate a snack at her desk.

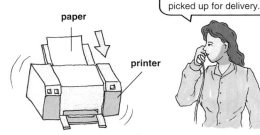

paper

printer

She printed some pages... (See p. 73.)

Hello. I have a package to be picked up for delivery.

...and called a courier. (See p. 56.)

Later, she turned off the lights...

EXIT

...and left the office.

Leaving the Office

Key Vocabulary

VERBS

be [was] out	set [set] down
check	show
find [found]	sign in
leave [left]	sign out
move	take [took]
print	write [wrote]
punch	
punch in	
punch out	
put [put]	
put back	

NOUNS

board	rack
card	sign-in book
clock	slot
column	system
date	time
in/out board	time card
line	time clock
marker	
name	
office	
pen	

OTHERS

else (adv.)
magnetic (adj.)

1. With an In/Out Board

Matt found his name on the board.

He moved his magnetic marker...

...to the "out" column.

Now, the board showed that Matt was out.

For Special Attention

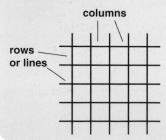

- **Magnetic** things stick to some kinds of metal.
- In a chart or table, there are **columns** and **rows** (or lines).

columns

rows or lines

- to **check** a clock = to look quickly at it to find out the time
- to **be out** = to not be in the office
- **someone else** = a different person
- "Albert **punched out**" = Albert punched his card to show he was out.

2. With a Sign-in System

In the sign-in book...

...Alice found the line where she had signed in.

She checked the clock...

...and wrote the time in the "out" column.

She set the pen down...

...and someone else signed out.

3. With a Punch-in System

Albert took his time card from the rack.

He put it into the slot on the time clock.

The time clock punched his card...

...by printing the date and time.

Albert put his card back in the rack.

Then someone else punched out.

14 Taking Directions

Key Vocabulary

VERBS
ask
come [came] up
explain
give [gave]
highlight
listen
make [made] sure
nod
take [took] notes
write [wrote] down

NOUNS
assignment
date
deadline
desk
detail
directions
information
material
note
supervisor

ADJECTIVE
new

For Special Attention

- An **assignment** is a job given to someone. Other ways of saying "an assignment" are "a task," "a project," and "some work."
- **materials** = things you need or use in completing a task
- When you **make sure of something**, you check to be certain you understand or know something.
- A **detail** is a fact or small piece of information.
- A **deadline** is the date or time something must be finished.

Hi, Matt. Can I speak with you?

Of course.

Matt's supervisor came up to his desk.

I'd like a summary of last month's sales data.

She explained a new assignment,...

These are the files you'll need.

...and gave him some materials.

Are these the daily sales figures?

Matt made sure of the details.

Yes, and these figures...

His supervisor highlighted some information.

...are the most recent.

Matt nodded as he listened,...

survey whole district sales

...and took notes.

When would you like the summary?

Next Tuesday would be great.

He asked when the deadline was...

Assignment due Tuesday 6 March

...and then wrote down the date.

Key Vocabulary

VERBS
ask
call
do [did]
estimate
explain
finish
have [had]
leave [left]
meet [met]
need
point out
report
show

NOUNS
coworker
help
information
problem
progress
schedule
supervisor
work

ADVERBIAL
so far

For Special Attention

- When you **report** on your **progress**, you tell how much you have finished and what you have left to do. This is often called a **progress report.**
- If something is done **on schedule**, it means it is finished on time–when it was planned to be finished.
- When you **estimate** something, you guess about a number–how much, how long, etc.

How's the project going?

It's going well.

Matt met with his supervisor to report on his progress.

I'm about half finished.

He showed her the work he'd done so far...

I'm not sure which of these forms is correct...

This one.

...and pointed out a problem.

...and there are some pages missing.

He also needed more information...

Would you please bring the February sales file to Matt?

...so his supervisor called a coworker for help.

Tomorrow I'll talk to Albert about this.

Then Matt explained what he had left to do...

Will you be done on time?

...and his supervisor asked if he would finish on schedule.

Tuesday. It shouldn't be a problem.

Wonderful.

Matt estimated when he would finish.

Key Vocabulary

VERBS
approve
attend
chair
close
come [came]
distribute
doodle
give [gave] (a presentation)
make [made] (an
  announcement)
move
open (a meeting)
raise (a hand)
sit [sat]
take [took] minutes
take notes
take the floor
take up
thank
whisper
yawn

NOUNS
agenda
announcement
boss
business
copy
discussion
end
floor
hand
head (of a table)
item
meeting
minutes
notepad
participant
people
presentation
table

ADJECTIVES
first
last
new
next

Before the meeting,
Alice distributed copies...

...of the agenda and the minutes
of the last meeting.

head of table

Okay. Shall we
get started?

Her boss chaired the meeting,
so he sat at the head of the table.

He opened the meeting...

Thank you for
being here.

All in favor of approving
the minutes?

**raised
hands**

...by thanking people for coming.

The participants approved the
minutes of the last meeting.

For Special Attention

- **agenda** = list of things to do or talk about
- If you **chair a meeting**, you run it; you start it, choose speakers, close it, etc.
- **approve** = say something is okay
- **take up an item** = begin to talk about it
- **take the floor** = become the person speaking at a meeting
- **presentation** = a set of things planned in advance and presented to a group
- **discussion** = talking about something, among two or more people
- **whisper** = speak very quietly
- If you **doodle**, you draw meaningless things on a piece of paper.

Alice's boss made a few announcements.

Then he took up the first item of new business on the agenda.

Alice took minutes. (See p. 36.)

One of the people at the meeting took the floor...

...and gave a presentation.

After some discussion...

...they moved to the next item.

During meetings, some people...

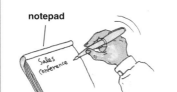

take notes

whisper to each other

At the end, he closed the meeting.

yawn

doodle

Key Vocabulary

VERBS

amend
approve
ask
come [came]
end
make [made]
  corrections
note
open
read [read] back
record
repeat
re-read [re-read]

say [said]
summarize
take [took]
  minutes
take out
type up
write [wrote]
  down

NOUNS

adjournment
business
correction
date
item
list
meeting
minutes
name
notepad
note

part
participant
people
person
remark
set
speaker
thing
time

OTHERS

last (adj.)
off the record (adv.)

For Special Attention

- **note** = notice (and record)
- **read back** = read to someone what you wrote down of their speech
- **amended** = changed
- **record** = write down
- **summarize** = write the main ideas in fewer words
- **off the record** = not to be included in an official document
- **re-read** = read again

Alice took out a notepad.

She wrote down names as people came into the meeting.

When the meeting opened...

...she noted the time.

She made corrections to the minutes of the last meeting...

...and read the corrections back.

Then the minutes were approved as amended.

Alice recorded what people said during the meeting...

...by summarizing their remarks.

Sometimes she asked people to repeat things.

Sometimes people said things off the record...

...so she did not write them down.

When the meeting ended, she noted the time.

Later, she re-read her notes...

...and typed up the minutes.

A Set of Minutes

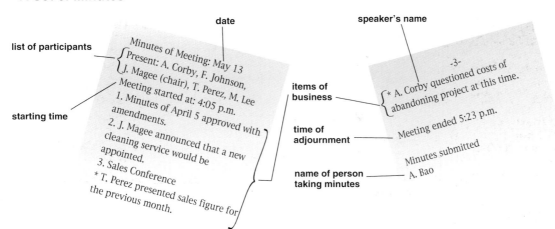

date

speaker's name

list of participants

Minutes of Meeting: May 13
Present: A. Corby, F. Johnson,
J. Magee (chair), T. Perez, M. Lee
Meeting started at: 4:05 p.m.
1. Minutes of April 5 approved with amendments.
2. J. Magee announced that a new cleaning service would be appointed.
3. Sales Conference
* T. Perez presented sales figure for the previous month.

starting time

items of business

-3-
* A. Corby questioned costs of abandoning project at this time.

Meeting ended 5:23 p.m.

time of adjournment

Minutes submitted
A. Bao

name of person taking minutes

Key Vocabulary

VERBS
distribute
make [made] copies
open
print out
proofread [proofread]
show
type up
write [wrote]

NOUNS
body
boss
copy
copy list
date
initials
list
memo
memo form
name
recipient
sender
subject
typist
word-processing
  software

For Special Attention

• A **memo**, or memorandum, is a note someone sends to other people in the same company. It is less formal than a letter.
• A **recipient** is someone who receives something.
• When you **proofread** something, you check it for mistakes.

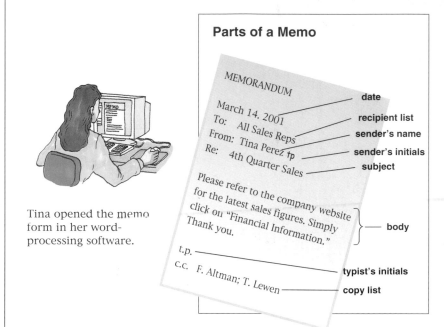

Parts of a Memo

MEMORANDUM

March 14. 2001

To: All Sales Reps   —— date
From: Tina Perez tp   —— recipient list
Re: 4th Quarter Sales —— sender's name
                          —— sender's initials
                          —— subject

Please refer to the company website for the latest sales figures. Simply click on "Financial Information."
Thank you.   —— body

t.p.
c.c. F. Altman; T. Lewen —— typist's initials
                           —— copy list

Tina opened the memo form in her word-processing software.

She typed up a memo...

...and printed it out.

Everything looks okay.

She proofread it...

Would you take a look at this, please?

...and showed it to her boss.

Then she made copies...

...and distributed them.

19 Leaving an Informal Note

Key Vocabulary

VERBS
add
be [was] away
call
jot down
leave [left]
peel
pick up
return
see [saw]
sign
stick [stuck]
stop

NOUNS
bottom
chair
desk
message
name
note
notepad
pad
paper
pen
piece
time

ADJECTIVES
informal
self-adhesive
short

For Special Attention

- An **informal** note is more relaxed and usually shorter than a letter or memo.
- One kind of **self-adhesive** notepaper is the Post-It® note. Post-It® is a registered trademark of 3M.
- When someone **is away**, they have left, usually for a short time.
- When you **jot** something down, you write it quickly.

Hmm? I wonder when he'll be back.

Alice stopped at Matt's desk, but he was away...

...so she picked up a self-adhesive notepad and pen...

...and jotted down a short message for Matt.

She added the time to the note.

Then she signed her name at the bottom...

...and peeled the piece of paper off the pad.

She stuck the note on Matt's chair so he would see it.

Matt here. I just saw your note.

When Matt returned, he called her.

управляет

20 Making Photocopies

Key Vocabulary

VERBS
adjust
align
clear
close
collate
enlarge
enter
feed [fed]
lift
make [made]
make copies
place
press
put [put]
reduce
sort
stack
take [took]
take off
take out
want

NOUNS
button
copy
darkness
document
feeder
glass
lid
machine
number
original
page
photocopier
photocopy
setting
size
start button
tray

OTHERS
crosswise (adv.)
darker (adj.)
face-down (adv.)
lighter (adj.)
multi-page (adj.)
one at a time (adverbial)

1 Tina lifted the lid of the photocopier.

2 She placed a document face-down on the glass...

выровняла

3 ...and aligned it. *выровнила*

4 Then she closed the lid.

скопировал
установила

5 She adjusted the settings to enlarge the copy...

данные

6 ...and entered the number of copies she wanted.

PHOTOCOPIER SETTINGS

size	enlarging	reducing
darkness	making a darker copy	making a lighter copy

sort

When the machine sorts, it feeds each copy into a different tray.

and

collate

When the machine collates, it puts the many pages of a document together—a full copy in each tray.

комплектовал *подавать материал*

1 She pressed the start button.

The machine made the copies...

...and fed them into the tray.

подкос лоток

  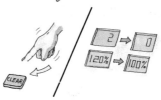 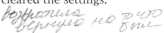

направила подала

Tina took her original off the glass... *убрала с*

...and took the copies out of the tray.

She cleared the settings.

возвратила вернула на то что было

Then she put a multi-page document in the feeder.

подающий механизм

She pressed a button so the machine would sort and collate the copies.

The machine fed in one page at a time...

...and sorted and collated the copies.

She took the copies out of the trays...

...and stacked them crosswise.

For Special Attention

- **Photocopying** is sometimes called "copying." The photocopier is also a "copier."
- **face-down** = with its front side down. The opposite is "face-up."
- **align** = put in the right position; line up
- An **original** is the thing you want to make copies of.

- A **document** is a written thing.
- A photocopier has **buttons**, NOT keys.
- The shiny, clear surface of a photocopier is called **"the glass."**
- When you **clear** the settings, the machine gets rid of your special instructions. The machine returns to its usual settings.

- **multi-page** = having many pages
- **one page at a time** = first one page, then another, then another
- **crosswise** = with one set facing in a different direction from the set under it

21 Dealing with Photocopier Problems

Key Vocabulary

VERBS

add	get [got]
break [broke]	open
down	pull out
call	put [put]
clean	reach
clear	refill
close	remove
come [came]	say [said]
come out	see [saw]
deal [dealt]	show
with	turn
find [found]	work
fix	work on

NOUNS

display	problem
glass	repair person
jam	repair service
knob	roller
machine	sheet
maintenance	sign
panel	smudge
paper	streak
paper jam	toner
paper tray	tool
photocopier	toolbox

OTHERS

completely (adv.)
front (adj.)
inside (adv.)
jammed (adj.)
out-of-order (adj.)
serious (adj.)

For Special Attention

- When there's a **jam**, something doesn't move through.
- **Panels** are flat pieces on the outside of a machine.
- One piece of paper is a **sheet.**
- **cleared** = gone, out of the way
- **toner** = dark powder in a photocopier
- **break down** = break so that it doesn't work anymore
- For machines, **work** = run.
- **work on X** = try to fix X

1. Removing Jammed Paper

The display said there was a paper jam.

Tina opened the front panel,...

...found one jammed sheet...

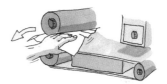

...and pulled the paper out.

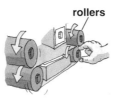

She couldn't see the other sheets...

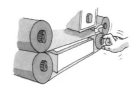

...so she turned a knob...

rollers

...to turn some rollers.

The paper came out.

Then, she reached inside to get another jammed sheet.

She closed the panels.

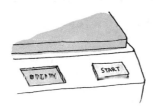
The display showed that the jam was cleared...

...and the machine worked again.

2. Other Photocopier Maintenance

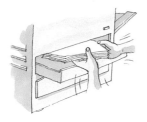
refilling the paper tray

adding toner

streak
smudge
cleaning the glass

3. Dealing with a Serious Problem

It won't work at all.

The photocopier broke down completely.

Tina put an "out-of-order" sign on it.

Could you send someone to fix our copier?

She called a repair service.

Hi, I'm here to fix the copier.

A repair person came,...

toolbox
tools
...worked on the machine...

Okay. It's running now.   Thanks.

...and fixed it.

Collating and Stapling

to collate - to arrange things such as papers in the right order

Key Vocabulary

VERBS

collate	reload
count	remove
go [went] in	run [ran]
grab	out of
have [had]	slip into
lay [laid] out	stack
lick	staple
pick up	
put [put]	

NOUNS

corner	stapler
extra	table
forefinger	thumb
page	tongue
pile	top
report	
set	
sheet	
spring	
staple	
staple remover	

OTHERS

crosswise (adv.)
easily (adv.)
empty (adj.)
full (adj.)
in order (adv.)
left-hand (adj.)
upper (adj.)
wrong (adv.)

Albert laid out the pages of the report...

...in order on a table.

He collated them by picking up one sheet from each pile...

...and putting one sheet on top of another.

He stacked the full sets crosswise.
набор

For Special Attention

- **in order** = from smallest to largest, largest to smallest, first to last, last to first, etc.
- There are many sheets of paper in a **stack** or **pile.**
- You **lick your fingers** to get them wet. Paper sticks easily to wet fingers.
- If you **run out of** something, you have no more. If you have **extras** of it, you have more than you need.
- **slip papers into a stapler** = put them into the open part of the stapler
- **reload a stapler** = refill it with staples

a full set - all the pages together

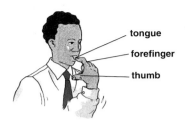

Sometimes he licked his thumb and forefinger...

...so he could grab sheets more easily.

He ran out of some pages...

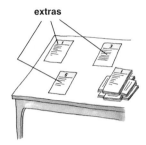

...while he still had extras of others.

He counted the sets.

He slipped each set into a stapler...

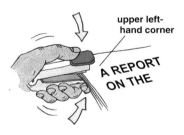

...and stapled the set in the upper left-hand corner.

When the stapler was empty...

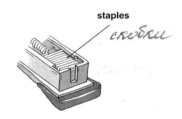

...he reloaded it.

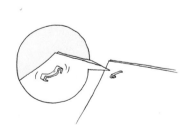

When a staple went in wrong,...

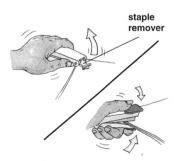

...he removed it and stapled the set again.

Key Vocabulary

VERBS

align
bind [bound]
bundle
clip
close
corner-staple
empty
keep [kept]
  together
make [made]
open
press
punch
put [put]

side-staple
slip
take [took]
use

NOUNS

3-ring binder
binder
bow
edge
folder
hole
label
page
paper clip
paper punch

pocket
punch
ribbon
ring
rubber band
scraps
spine
staple
string
tab

ADVERB

together

For Special Attention

• **Rubber bands** stretch.

⬭ ➝ ⬭

• **align** = line up; get
  something straight
• A **punch** punches holes. You
  can also say that you punch
  holes with a punch.
• A **spine** is the closed **edge** of
  a book, folder or binder.

Some Ways of Keeping Pages Together

to bind скреплять
делать дырки

paper clip скрепка

clipping them together
скреплять скрепкой

to band свертка

using rubber bands

staples — скобка

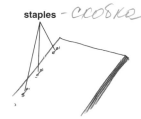

side-stapling them

staple

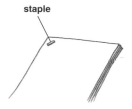

corner-stapling them
(see p. 44)

folder

pocket

putting them in a folder

bow

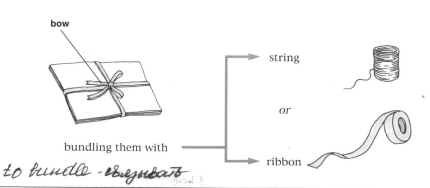

bundling them with

string

or

ribbon

to bundle - связывать

Using a Punch and 3-Ring Binders

Albert took a few pages,...

...aligned them in a paper punch...

...and pressed on the punch.

(three-hole punch

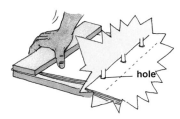

It made 3 holes along the edge of the pages.

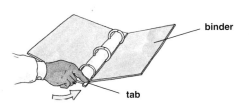

Albert pressed the tab in a 3-ring binder...

...to open the rings.

He slipped some pages onto the rings.

He pressed the rings together...

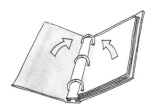

...to close them.

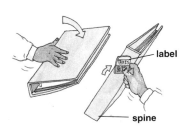

He closed the binder and put a label on its spine.

Then he emptied the paper scraps out of the punch.

Key Vocabulary

VERBS

arrange	put [put]
close	re-file
file	set [set] up
flip through	stick [stuck]
get [got]	type
have [had]	
need	
open	
pull out	

NOUNS

alphabetical order	label
	name
customer	paper
document	piece
drawer	tab
file	
filing cabinet	
folder	
hanging file	

OTHERS

alphabetically (adv.)
color-coded (adj.)
legal-size (adj.)
letter-size (adj.)
new (adj.)

For Special Attention

- **arrange** = put in order, according to a pattern
- You **flip through** files by using your fingers to push them quickly forward.
- **re-file** = file again
- **file** = the folder and the papers in it
- **file folder** = the case that contains the papers
- File folders that are a very light brown are called "**manila folders.**"
- The **tab** of a file folder sticks out from the rest of the folder.

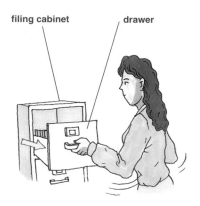

filing cabinet   drawer

alphabetical order: A, B, C, D...

Tina opened a drawer of the filing cabinet.

The files were arranged alphabetically.

этикетка, ярлык

tab

She flipped through the files...

...and pulled out the one she needed.

She opened the folder,...

...put a piece of paper into it,...

...closed the folder...

...and re-filed it.

Setting up a New File

Tina had to file something about a new customer.

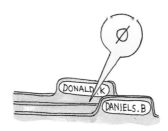

There was no file for him yet.

She got a new folder.

She typed the customer's name on a label...

...and stuck the label on the tab of the folder.

Then she filed the folder.

Kinds of Files

legal-size folder

letter-size folder

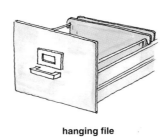

hanging file

color-coded files

25 Receiving and Distributing Mail

Key Vocabulary

VERBS

arrive	put [put]
attach	receive
check	remove
clear	slide [slid]
deliver	sort
distribute	stamp
drop	take [took]
fold	toss
give [gave]	unfold
hand	
look	
look through	
open	

NOUNS

bottom	paper clip
box	person
coworker	pile
date	stack
department	stamp
desk	wrapper
enclosure	
envelope	
junk mail	
letter	
letter opener	
magazine	
mail	
mail cart	
mail clerk	
mailbox	
outgoing mail	

ADJECTIVES

big
confidential
outgoing

For Special Attention

Checking a Mailbox

Matt looked in his box.

He removed a stack of mail.

He looked through the mail...

...and tossed out junk mail.

Then he put an envelope into a coworker's mailbox.

Another envelope was too big,...

...so he folded it...

...and slid it in.

He dropped some mail into the outgoing mailbox.

- In an office mailroom, a **mailbox** and a **mail slot** are the same. Another name for it is "pigeonhole."
- **Junk mail** is unwanted mail. Often it is advertising.

- **Interoffice mail** is delivered to different offices within the same company.
- **Outgoing mail** is to be delivered outside the company.
- **Incoming mail** is delivered to your company.

- A **department** is one part or area of a company.
- An **enclosure** is something extra included with a letter or memo.
- Something is **confidential** if it is meant to be private or secret.

Receiving and Distributing Mail from a Mail Cart

The mail clerk arrived with the mail cart.

He handed the mail for the department to Alice.

She gave him her outgoing mail.

Then she cleared her desk...

...and sorted the mail for each person.

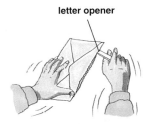

She opened the envelopes...

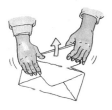

...and removed the letters and enclosures.

After she unfolded the letters...

...she stamped the date received on them...

...and attached the enclosures with paper clips.

She took the wrappers off magazines...

...and put them on the bottom of each pile.

She didn't open "confidential" mail.

Finally, she delivered the mail to her coworkers.

51

VERBS

add	proofread
address	[proofread]
collect	put [put]
correct	seal
find [found]	sign
finish	staple
fold	tape
insert	type
label	wrap
lick	
mail	
pack	
prepare	
print out	

NOUNS

address label	label
attachment	letter
body	letterhead
box	package
bubble wrap	return
closing	address
computer	salutation
dateline	
enclosure	
enclosure	
notification	
envelope	
equipment	
error	
flap	
inside address	
item	

ADJECTIVE
shut

Preparing a Letter to be Mailed

Alice finished typing a letter on her computer.

After she printed it out...

...she proofread it for errors.

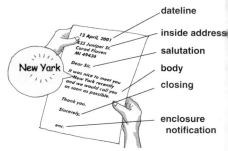

dateline
inside address
salutation
body
closing
enclosure notification

She found an error...

...and corrected it.

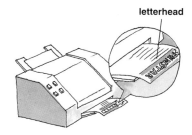

letterhead

She printed it out on letterhead.

- When you **proofread** something, you check it for mistakes.
- **letterhead** = paper that has a company's name, address, etc. printed on it in a nicely designed way
- The **return address** shows who sent the letter or piece of mail.
- An **attachment** is stapled or clipped to a letter. An **enclosure** goes in the same envelope as a letter but is not attached to the letter.
- When you **seal** something, you close it tightly.

She signed it.

She addressed an envelope...

...and added a label for the return address.

She stapled an attachment to the letter,...

...folded the letter and attachment...

...and inserted them into the envelope.

Then she collected some enclosures...

...and put them into the envelope.

She licked the flap of the envelope...

...and sealed it.

Preparing a Package to Be Mailed

Alice wrapped the equipment in bubble wrap.

She packed it in a box.

Then she taped the box shut...

...and labeled it with an address label.

Key Vocabulary

VERBS

apply
come [came] out
give [gave]
hit [hit]
look
moisten
place
press
push
put [put]

see [saw]
send [sent] out
show
slide [slid]
stamp
tear [tore] out
use
weigh

NOUNS

basket
button
display
"enter" button
envelope
first class mail
international mail
label
machine
mail
mail clerk
package
parcel
piece
postage

postage label
postage meter
postage rate chart
postage scale
postage stamp
"print" button
slot
stamp
stamp booklet

ADJECTIVES

correct
large
thick
outgoing

Using a Postage Scale and a Postage Meter

Matt put an envelope on the postage scale.

He pushed the button for first class mail.

The display showed the postage.

He pushed the buttons on the postage meter...

...and hit the "enter" button.

He placed the envelope in the slot,...

...and slid it through.

The machine stamped it with the correct postage.

For Special Attention

- A **postage scale** is an electronic machine which tells how much a piece of mail weighs and how much postage it needs.
- A **postage meter** puts postage on thinner envelopes and supplies postage labels for bigger pieces of mail.
- When you **moisten** something, you get it slightly wet.
- Another word for **metered mail** is "franked mail."

Next Matt weighed a large, thick parcel.

He pressed the "print" button on the machine.

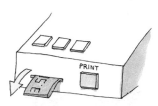

A postage label came out of the machine.

Matt applied the label to the package.

Then he put all his mail in the "outgoing" basket.

Using Postage Stamps

Alice weighed a piece of international mail.

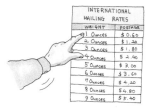

She looked at the postage rate chart to see the postage.

INTERNATIONAL MAILING RATES	
WEIGHT	POSTAGE
1 Ounces	$0.60
2 Ounces	$1.20
3 Ounces	$1.80
4 Ounces	$2.40
5 Ounces	$3.00
6 Ounces	$3.60
7 Ounces	$4.20
8 Ounces	$4.80
9 Ounces	$5.40

Then she tore some stamps out of a stamp booklet,...

...moistened the stamps...

...and put them on the envelope.

Later, she gave the mail to the mail clerk.

28 Using an Express Delivery Service

Key Vocabulary

VERBS

add	move around
arrive	pack
ask	pay [paid]
bring [brought]	pick up
call	receive
check	seal
drop off	stick [stuck]
fill out	take [took]
gather	tear [tore] off
give [gave]	use
have [had]	want
keep [kept]	weigh
measure	

NOUNS

box	packing
chart	material
city	pickup
clerk	receipt
counter	scale
customer copy	service
day	status
delivery person	tape measure
delivery price	top
express delivery	waybill
file	
group	
kind	
office	
package	
packaging	
tape	

ADJECTIVE

next

For Special Attention

Having a Package Picked Up at the Office

Alice gathered a group of files to go to another city.

She packed them in a box...

...and added packing material to keep them from moving around.

scale

Then she weighed...

tape measure

...and measured the box.

She filled out a waybill.

- When you **gather** things, you bring them together in one place.
- The **scale** shows the package's weight is 12.5 lbs. This is equal to about 5.5 kilograms. "lbs" means "pounds."
- Another name for a **waybill** is an **airbill**.
- The person who sends the express package gets the **customer copy** of a waybill. Other copies go to the shipper and the receiver.
- A **receipt** shows that you've paid for something.

packaging tape

Then she sealed the box...

...and stuck the waybill on.

I'd like to request a package pickup, please.

Next, she called the express delivery service for a pickup.

When the delivery person arrived,...

...he took the package from Alice,...

...tore the customer copy off the top of the waybill...

...and gave it to Alice.

My tracking number is 02007.

Your package arrived this morning.

The next day, Alice checked the status of her package.

Dropping Off a Package at the Express Delivery Office

Matt brought a package to the express delivery office.

He checked a chart for delivery prices.

He filled out the waybill...

...and brought the package to the counter.

Would you like two-day or overnight delivery?

Two-day service is fine.

The clerk asked him what kind of service he wanted.

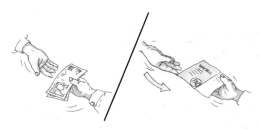

Matt paid the clerk and received his receipt.

29 Receiving an Express Package

Key Vocabulary

VERBS
arrive
be [was] supposed to
call
deal [dealt] with
fill out
get [got]
hand
make [made] sure
open
receive
remove
report
return
say [said]
see [saw]
send [sent]
sign for
trace

NOUNS
claim form
company
contents
customer service
damage
delivery
delivery person
express delivery
information
morning
package
problem
product
representative
sender

ADJECTIVES
broken   lost
damaged   missing
express   next
late

For Special Attention

- When you **sign for** a package, you are saying that you have received it.
- The **contents** of a package are the things inside.

- You fill out a **claim form** when there is a problem with your delivery, for example if something is damaged or missing from the box.

- A **tracking number** helps delivery companies **locate** or find missing packages.
- To **trace** something means to follow it to try to find it.

Receiving a Package

A delivery person arrived with a package for Matt.

Matt signed for the package...

...and the delivery person handed it to him.

After Matt opened it,...

...he removed the contents.

He made sure nothing was missing or broken.

58

Dealing with Delivery Problems: Product Damage

When Alice opened an express delivery package,...

...she saw that the contents were damaged.

She called the delivery company to report it.

The customer service representative said he'd send a claim form.

Later, Alice filled out the claim form...

...and returned it to the delivery company.

Dealing with Delivery Problems: A Late or Lost Package

Matt's package didn't arrive when it was supposed to...

...so he called the sender to get more information about the package.

Next Matt called the delivery company...

...to trace the package.

The next morning, Matt's package arrived.

30 Finding Telephone Numbers

Key Vocabulary

VERBS
call
check
dial
do [did] a
  search
find [found]
flip through
give [gave]
look
look up

run [ran]
take [took] out
tell [told]
want
write [wrote]
  down

NOUNS
address book
area code
directory
  assistance
finger
Internet
list
listing
long distance
name
number
operator

page
phone book
phone number
rotary file
search
telephone
  directory
telephone
  number
yellow pages

OTHERS
down (adv.)
right (adj.)

For Special Attention

- If you **flip through** a book, you turn its pages quickly.
- A **long distance call** is made to a number far away.
- **Local calls** are made to numbers near you.
- A **listing** is the name of a person or business as it is written in the phone book.
- A **yellow pages** directory contains advertisements for businesses and services. A **white pages** directory contains only phone numbers and addresses for people and businesses.

Looking Up a Number in a Phone Book

Albert took out a telephone directory.

He flipped through the pages...

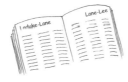

...until he found the right page.

He ran his finger down the list of names...

...and wrote down Ann Lee's number.

Calling Directory Assistance

Albert dialed long distance directory assistance.

A New York listing for James Dent, please.

He told the operator the listing he wanted.

The number is **212**-555-3131.

area code

As she gave him the number, he wrote it down.

Other Ways to Find Phone Numbers

address book

rotary file

look in an
address book

look in a
rotary file

check the
yellow pages

do a search on
the Internet

Key Vocabulary

VERBS
answer
call
end
flash
give [gave]
hang [hung] up
identify
listen
pick up
push down
ring [rang]
say [said] goodbye
take [took] notes

NOUNS
button
call
caller
conversation
name
phone
phone line
reason
receiver
telephone
telephone call

For Special Attention

- For the parts of a telephone, see p. 18.
- A **flashing** light on a phone shows a call that hasn't been answered.
- When you **identify yourself,** you tell who you are. Each company has its own way for employees to identify themselves when they answer the phone.

---

phone line

rrringg

As Alice's phone rang, one of the phone line buttons flashed.

Alice pushed the button down and...

Accounting.
This is Alice .

...picked up the receiver to answer the phone.

After Alice identified herself,...

Hi, Alice. This is Matt from Marketing. I'm looking for an annual report.

...the caller gave his name and reason for calling.

Alice listened and took notes.

Thank you, Alice. Goodbye.

You're welcome. Goodbye.

They ended their conversation by saying goodbye...

...and Alice hung up the telephone.

Key Vocabulary

VERBS

answer	pick up
ask	push down
call	ring [rang]
dial	speak [spoke]
explain	
hear [heard]	
identify	
listen	
look up	
make [made]	
a call	

NOUNS

button
dial tone
directory
number
phone
phone line
phone number
receiver
secretary
telephone call
telephone directory

ADJECTIVE

open

For Special Attention

- An **open phone line** is one that isn't being used. The button for this line is unlit, or dark.
- A **dial tone** is a sound that tells you the phone is ready to use.
- A **secretary** is a person who works as an assistant to someone in a company. One of the secretary's jobs can include answering the phone.

---

telephone directory

1
004

Tina looked up Mr. King's phone number in the directory.

009

She pushed down a button on her phone for an open phone line,...

014

...picked up the receiver...

mmmm

...and heard the dial tone.

018

She dialed Mr. King's number.

rrringg

023

Then she listened as the phone rang.

Good morning. Mr. King's office.

031

Mr. King's secretary answered the phone.

Hello. This is Tina Perez from Denstar.

Tina identified herself...

Is Mr. King in?

...and asked to speak to Mr. King.

Bob King.

Hello. Mr. King. This is Tina Perez calling to confirm our lunch.

Tina explained why she called.

Key Vocabulary

VERBS
announce
begin [began]
dial
give [gave]
hang [hung] up
look up
push
put [put] (X) on hold
speak [spoke]
transfer

NOUNS
button
call
caller
company directory
extension
"hold" button
number
phone
"transfer" button

ADVERBIAL
on hold

For Special Attention

- When you **transfer** a call, you move it from one telephone (number) to another.
- When you are **on hold,** you are waiting for someone or something.
- An **extension** is a person's phone number inside a company. It has fewer numbers than a regular phone number.

Please hold, I will transfer your call.

Alice put the caller on hold by pushing the "hold" button.

extension number

She looked up Albert's extension in the company directory.

Albert's extension is 9989. I'll transfer you.

She gave the caller Albert's extension.

"transfer" button

She pushed the "transfer" button on her phone...

...and dialed Albert's extension.

Hi, Albert. I have a caller who needs your help.

She announced the call to Albert.

Then she hung up...

Hi. This is Albert. How may I help you?

...and Albert began speaking with the caller.

34 Taking a Message

Key Vocabulary

VERBS
answer
ask
fill out
hang [hung] up
identify
offer
pick up
put [put]
say [said]
spell
take [took] a message
tell [told]
write [wrote]

NOUNS
caller   phone
desk   telephone
form   number
information
last name
message
name
pen

ADJECTIVE
available

For Special Attention

- Someone who is **available** is free to speak with you or see you. If he/she is **not available,** he/she may be busy or somewhere else.
- A **form** is a printed piece of paper with spaces to write information. When you **fill out** a form, you write information in the spaces.
- Your **last name** is also called your "family name" or "surname." In this example, the caller's last name is "Breen" and his first name, or given name, is "Joe."

Marketing. This is Tina.

Tina answered the phone.

Hello. Is Jim Beck in?

The caller asked for someone.

I'm sorry. He's left for the day. Can I take a message?

Tina said he wasn't available and offered to take a message.

She picked up a pen and message form.

This is Joe Breen with XYZ Company.

The caller identified himself.

Can you spell your last name, sir?

That's B-R-E-E-N.

She asked the caller to spell his last name.

She wrote the information on a form.

Ask him to call me at 555-7428.

Then the caller told her his telephone number.

Tina filled out more of a form...

...and hung up.

She put the message on Mr. Beck's desk.

Key Vocabulary

VERBS
ask
call
explain
give [gave]
identify
leave [left]
return
say [said]
say goodbye
speak [spoke]
spell
tell [told]
thank
want

NOUNS
call
message
name
office
phone number
secretary

ADJECTIVE
available

For Special Attention

• If you ask someone to **return** your call, you would like them to call you back.
• If you leave a message on someone's **voice mail** or **answering machine,** after you hear the "beep" you would give the same information you would tell a secretary.

Hello. May I speak with Laura Smith, please?

Albert asked to speak to someone.

I'm sorry. She's in a meeting right now.

The secretary said she was not available...

Would you like to leave a message, sir?

...and asked if Albert wanted to leave a message.

Yes. My name is Albert Turner from Denstar.

Albert identified himself...

That's T-U-R-N-E-R.

...and spelled his name.

I can be reached at 555-7799.

Then he gave her his phone number.

I'm calling about the report she sent me.

He explained why he called...

Will you please have her return my call?

...and asked that Ms. Smith return his call.

I'll be in my office until 5:00.

He told the secretary when he would be in his office.

Thank you very much! Goodbye.

You're welcome. Goodbye.

Then he thanked her and said goodbye.

36 Sending a Fax

Key Vocabulary

VERBS
come [came] out
dial
feed [fed]
load
prepare
press
remove
scan
send [sent]
show

NOUNS
cover sheet
display
document
document feeder
document return tray
fax
fax machine
fax number
number keys
page
paper
recipient
"send" button
tray

OTHERS
face down (adv.)
ready (adj.)

For Special Attention

• The word **fax** is the shortened form of "facsimile."
• The word **fax** can be both a noun and a verb. Therefore, you can "**send a fax**," and "**fax a document**."
• The **cover sheet** shows who the fax should go to after it arrives and how many pages are included.
• The **recipient** is the person to whom the fax is sent. The fax comes from the **sender**.
• When the fax machine **scans** the document, it is similar to taking a picture of it.

Alice prepared a cover sheet.

She loaded the papers face-down.

The display showed "ready."

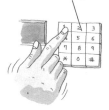

She dialed the recipient's fax number...

...and pressed the "send" button.

The pages fed into the fax machine,...

...were scanned...

...and came out into the document return tray.

Alice removed the document from the tray.

Key Vocabulary

VERBS
beep
begin [began]
check
deliver
enter
receive
remove
see [saw]
show
staple
stop

NOUNS
display
exit tray
fax
fax machine
machine
page
recipient

OTHERS
illegible (adj.)
incoming (adj.)
legible (adj.)
missing (adj.)
together (adv.)

For Special Attention

- Something that is **incoming** is arriving. Something that is leaving is **"outgoing."**
- If something is **missing**, it can't be found.
- Something that is **illegible** is very difficult to read.
- A **recipient** is the person who receives a fax.

The fax machine beeped...

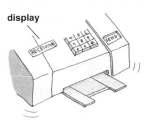

...and the display showed an incoming fax.

Pages began to enter the machine's exit tray.

When the machine stopped, Alice removed the pages.

Looks like everything's here.

legible   illegible

She checked to see if any pages were missing or illegible.

Then she stapled the pages together...

...and delivered them to the recipient.

Key Vocabulary

VERBS

beep	put back
begin [began]	receive
call	refill
check	remove
clear	replace
close	say [said]
deal [dealt]	see [saw]
with	send [sent]
fan	separate
get [got]	show
look	stick [stuck]
open	stop
print	try
push down	want
put [put]	

NOUNS

cartridge	page
cover	paper
display	paper jam
document	paper tray
document	print
feeder	problem
fax	repair service
fax machine	stack
ink cartridge	supply cabinet
machine	user's manual

OTHERS

back (adv.)	light (adj.)
darker (adj.)	new (adj.)
empty (adj.)	other (adj.)
incoming (adj.)	together (adv.)
jammed (adj.)	

For Special Attention

- To **fan** something is to spread it out.
- A **stack** is a pile or group of things, one on top of another.
- To **replace** is to change one thing for another.
- A **cartridge** is a container that might be replaced or refilled.
- A **user's manual** is a book that gives you information about how to use and care for something.

1. Clearing a Paper Jam

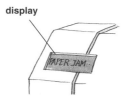

Matt wanted to send a fax...

...but the machine beeped and stopped.

The display said the paper was jammed.

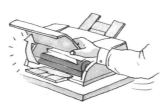

Matt opened the cover of the fax machine...

...and removed the document.

He saw that the pages were stuck together...

...so he separated them.

He closed the cover by pushing down on it.

Then he put the pages back in the document feeder to try again.

2. Refilling the Paper Tray

The display showed an incoming fax...

...but Matt didn't see a fax being printed...

...so he checked the paper tray and saw that it was empty.

He fanned a stack of new paper to separate the pages.

Then he refilled the paper tray...

...and the fax began printing.

3. Replacing the Ink Cartridge

The print on the fax Matt received was too light...

...so he opened the fax machine and removed the ink cartridge.

It was empty.

He got a new cartridge from the supply cabinet...

...and put it in the fax machine.

Then he printed the page and saw that the print was darker.

Other Ways to Deal with Fax Machine Problems

look in the user's manual

call a repair service

39

Starting a Computer

Key Vocabulary

VERBS

appear	start
begin [began]	step on
click on	turn on
flash	use
move	
open	
press	
see [saw]	

NOUNS

CD-ROM drive
computer
CPU
cursor
desk
floppy disk drive
icon
monitor
monitor screen
mouse
mouse pad
"on/off" button
pointer
power cord
power strip
program
screen
word-processing

For Special Attention

- A **power strip** is an electrical cord that contains multiple outlets. Several pieces of equipment may be plugged into one power strip at the same time.
- **Icons** are the small pictures on the monitor screen that represent computer programs and files.
- The **cursor** shows the place on the screen where what you type will appear.
- The **pointer** on the screen moves as you move the mouse.

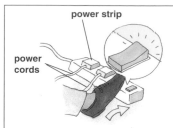

Alice stepped on the power strip beneath her desk,...

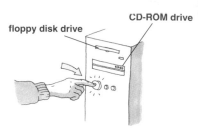

...pressed the "on/off" button on her CPU...

...and turned on her monitor.

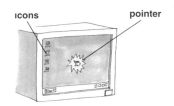

Alice saw icons appear on the screen and the pointer began to flash.

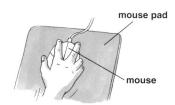

She used the mouse...

...to move the pointer to the word-processing icon.

She clicked on the icon...

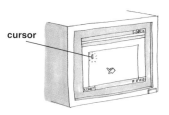

...and the program opened.

Shutting Down a Computer

Key Vocabulary

VERBS
ask
choose [chose]
click
close
go [went]
save
shut [shut] down
shut off
turn off
want
work on

NOUNS
computer
document
menu
monitor
option
power strip
program
prompt
screen
word-processing

ADJECTIVE
dark

For Special Attention

- To **shut** something **down** means to turn it off.
- An **option** is a choice.
- A **prompt** is the computer's way of asking for information from the user.
- When something **goes dark,** the lights go off.

Alice saved the document she was working on.

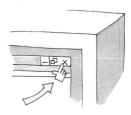

Then she closed the word-processing program.

When she chose the "shut down" option from the menu,...

...a prompt asked if she wanted to shut down the computer.

Alice clicked "OK",...

...and the computer shut off.

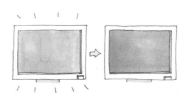

After the screen went dark,...

...Alice turned off the monitor and power strip.

Key Vocabulary

VERBS
begin [began]
check
hit [hit]
indent
key in
make [made]
name
open
press
save
space
type
use

NOUNS
capital letter
"enter" key
keyboard
line
program
report
"shift" key
space bar
spelling
tab key
text
word
word-processing

ADJECTIVE
new

For Special Attention

• A **capital letter** is also called an uppercase letter.

Alice opened the word processing program.

She began typing a report.

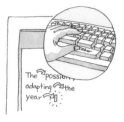

As she typed, she hit the space bar to space between words...

...and used the "shift" key to make a capital letter.

She pressed the "enter" key to begin a new line...

...and indented the new line with the tab key.

She checked the spelling.

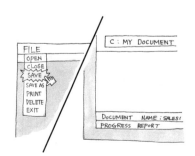

Then she saved and named the report.

Key Vocabulary

VERBS
add
click
preview
print
remove
save
set [set] up
turn on

NOUNS
copy
document
feeder
output tray
paper
paper guide
power button
print job
printer
report

ADJECTIVE
monthly

For Special Attention

- When you **preview a document**, you see what it will look like when it's printed.
- When you **set up something**, you are getting it ready.

That's done. Time to print.

power button

feeder   paper guides

After Alice saved her monthly report,...

...she turned on her printer.

She added paper to the feeder.

Then she previewed the document,...

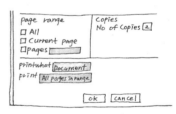

page range
☐ All
☐ Current page
☐ pages

Copies
No of copies 2

print what Document
print All pages in range

ok   cancel

...set up the print job...

OK   Cancel

CLICK!

...and clicked "OK."

After printing two copies of the report,...

output tray

...Alice removed them from the output tray.

Key Vocabulary

VERBS
check
close
delete
double-click
download
enter
exit
forward
list
open
print
read [read]
receive
reply
save

NOUNS
account
attachment
copy
e-mail
inbox
junk mail
message
password
program
sender
supervisor

ADJECTIVES
final
first
incoming
new
next
several

Albert opened his e-mail program to check his incoming messages.

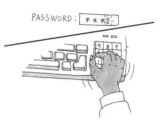

When he entered his password,...

...his inbox listed several new messages.

The first message was junk mail,...

...so Albert deleted it.

He double-clicked on the next message...

...and it opened.

For Special Attention

- A **password** is a secret word or expression that must be given before an e-mail account will open. When it is typed, the words and letters are shown as asterisks (***) on the screen.

- **Junk mail** is mail, often advertising, that you receive but haven't asked for. In e-mail, junk mail is also called **spam**.
- When you **forward** a message, you send it on to someone else.

- When you **download** a file, you copy it from the Internet onto your computer.
- An **attachment** is a document that is included with an e-mail.

Albert read the message...

...and forwarded it to his supervisor.

He closed the message and opened the next one.

He saved the next message.

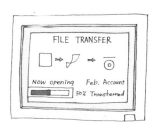

Then he downloaded an attachment...

...and printed a copy.

After reading the final message,...

...he replied to the sender.

Then he exited his e-mail account.

44 Sending E-mail

Key Vocabulary

VERBS

add	move
appear	open
attach	scroll
begin [began]	send [sent]
click on	start
exit	tell [told]
go [went]	type
hit [hit]	write [wrote]

NOUNS

account	message area
address	message
address book	window
copy list	name
e-mail	program
field	prompt
file	recipient
icon	scroll bar
list	subject line
mail	tab key
message	

ADJECTIVES

new
next

For Special Attention

- An **e-mail address book** is similar to a regular address book. It contains the Internet addresses of people to whom you regularly send messages.
- When you **scroll through** something on the computer, you make the information on the monitor screen move up, down, or sideways.
- A **recipient** is a person who receives something.
- On a computer screen, a **field** is a space you fill.
- People on your **copy list** get to see your message to someone else.
- If you **attach** a file, you add an already-written file to your e-mail message.

After Albert started his e-mail program,...

...he clicked on the icon to write a new message...,

...and a new message window opened.

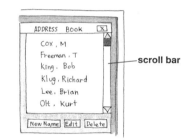

scroll bar

Albert opened his e-mail address book...

...and scrolled through the list of names.

He clicked on one recipient's name...

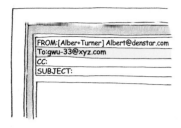

...and the address appeared above the new message window.

To go to the next field, Albert hit the tab key.

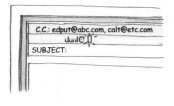

Then he added e-mail addresses to the copy list.

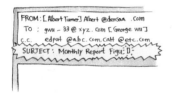

After he typed the subject line,...

...he moved to the message area and began typing.

He attached a file to the e-mail message.

I'll send this now.

Then he sent the message.

After a prompt told him the mail had been sent,...

That's enough for now.

...Albert exited his e-mail account.

Key Vocabulary

VERBS
click on
come [came] up
copy
download
exit
follow
get [got]
go [went] off line
go on line
list
look
open up
scroll
start
type in
wait
want

NOUNS

bookmark	page
browser	portal
button	program
hit	search
homepage	URL
icon	
information	
Internet	
keyword	
link	

OTHERS
interesting (adj.)
off line (adverbial)
on line (adverbial)

Albert clicked on an icon to open up his browser...

...and went on line.

He clicked on one of his bookmarks...

...and the page he wanted came up.

Then he typed in the URL for a portal...

...and typed in a keyword.

He clicked on a button to start his search.

For Special Attention

- **browser** = software that gets you into the Internet
- **go on line** = connect to a network
- **bookmark** = a URL saved in a special list because you want to use it often
- **URL** = an internet "address"
- **search** = the process of looking for something
- **portal** = software that helps take you to places on the Internet
- **keyword** = a word that is part of a phrase you want to find
- **hit** = a website found for you by a search engine
- You **scroll through** a file by making text move up or down as you read.
- To **download** something is to take it from a network and save it on a hard disk or floppy (or print it).

He waited a while.

The program listed some hits.

He clicked on one that looked interesting.

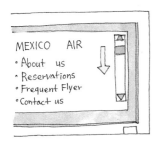

He scrolled through the homepage.

He followed links...

...to other pages.

He copied some information to download.

Then he exited the browser...

...and went off line.

Key Vocabulary

VERBS

address	set [set]
backspace	straighten
begin [began]	turn
center	turn on
complete	type
correct	use
feed [fed]	
finish	
hit [hit]	
loosen	
press	
pull out	
secure	

NOUNS

document	"return" key
envelope	"shift" key
error	title
form	typewriter
label	
letter	
"letter" key	
line	
margin	
paper	
paper release lever	
piece	
platen	
platen knob	

OTHERS

clockwise (adv.)
counterclockwise (adv.)
new (adj.)
upper case (adj.)

Alice turned on her typewriter.

platen

She centered a piece of paper in the platen...

platen knob

...and turned the platen knob clockwise to secure the paper.

Then she fed the paper into the typewriter with the "return" key.

That looks straight.

...and straightened the paper.

paper release lever

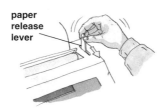

She loosened the paper release lever...

For Special Attention

- The **platen** is the roller of the typewriter.
- **center paper** = put it in the middle of the platen
- When you turn something in a **clockwise** direction, you turn it in the direction that a clock moves. The opposite of clockwise is **counterclockwise.**

- When you **secure** something, you close it tightly.
- **Margins** are the spaces along the edge of the paper.
- **Upper case** letters are also called **capital** letters. (See p. 72.) **Lower case** letters are the small forms of upper case or capital letters.

After she set the margins,...

...she typed the title of the document.

She hit "return" to begin a new line.

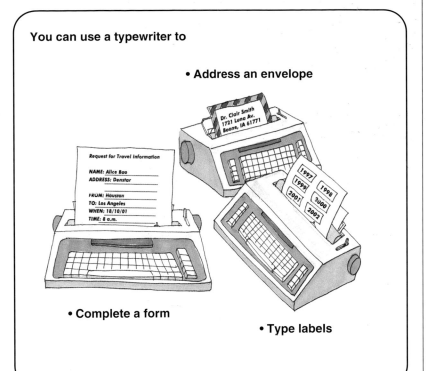

You can use a typewriter to

• **Address an envelope**

• **Complete a form**

• **Type labels**

Alice pressed the "shift" key and a "letter" key...

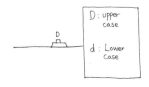

...to type an upper case letter.

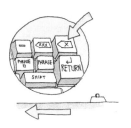

She backspaced...

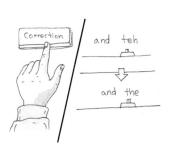

...and corrected an error.

When she was finished, she turned the platen knob counterclockwise...

...and pulled the paper out of the typewriter.

Key Vocabulary

VERBS

add	tear [tore] off
appear	total
attach	turn off
check	turn on
clear	use
discover	
enter	
feed [fed]	
open	
print	
subtract	

NOUNS

amount
calculator
decimal point
display
division key
error
file
keypad
minus key
multiplication key
number
paper roll
plus key
printout
receipt
result
tape
total key
work

ADVERB

together (adv.)

For Special Attention

- **Receipts** are slips of paper that show money has been paid for something.
- A **keypad** on a calculator can also be called a **keyboard.**
- When you **subtract** something, you take it away.
- When you **total** a group of numbers, you add them together to reach one amount.

Albert turned on his calculator.

Then he opened a file of receipts.

paper roll
display
plus key
minus key
multiplication key
division key
total key
keypad

As he entered the amounts from each receipt on the calculator keypad,...

...he added them together.

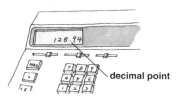

decimal point

The numbers appeared on the display...

...and were printed on the tape.

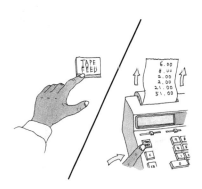

When he fed the tape up...

...and checked his work,...

...he discovered an error...

...so he subtracted an amount.

After he entered all the numbers from the receipts,...

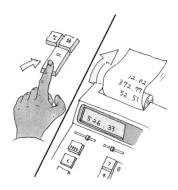

...he totaled the results.

Then he tore off the printout...

...and attached it to the receipts.

He cleared the display...

...and turned off the calculator.

48

Receiving an Invoice/Paying

Key Vocabulary

VERBS

attach
check
compare
confirm
deliver
file
issue
make [made] sure
order
pay [paid]
pull out
put [put]

receive
record
separate
sign
stamp

NOUNS

amount
boss
check
copy
customer
detail
envelope
invoice
item
office
outgoing mail

package
payment
price
product
purchase
  order
software
vendor

ADJECTIVES

correct
new
paid

For Special Attention

- A **vendor** is a person or company who sells something.
- An **invoice** is a bill.
- A **purchase order** is a request to buy something from a vendor, or seller of goods.
- When you **confirm** something, you make certain of it.
- When you **issue a check,** you prepare it in order to pay for something.
- When you **record** information, you write it down.

Receiving an Invoice

We'll buy 3 copies of Bitware 7000.

Great!

vendor

Alice's office ordered some new software.

It was delivered.

Please pay this amount

There was an invoice in the package.

Alice pulled out the invoice.

INVOICE

Please pay this amo

ITEM

BITCORP 2001
CABLE
MANUAL

She made sure that every item on the invoice...

Okay. That's here.

...had been delivered.

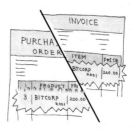

She compared the purchase order to the invoice...

...to check product details and prices.

Paying

That's OK.

After confirming that the invoice was correct,...

amount
$317.46

...Alice issued a check for the invoice amount... (See p. 86.)

...and her boss signed it.

She separated the copies of the invoice.

Then she stamped the customer's copy "paid"...

...and recorded the payment details.

She attached the check to the vendor's copy,...

...put them in an envelope,...

OUT GOING

...and put the envelope in the outgoing mail.

Then she filed the customer's copy.

49 Issuing a Check

Key Vocabulary

VERBS
click on
enter
fill out
issue
open
print out
sign
tear [tore] out
write [wrote] out

NOUNS
account
amount
boss
check
computer
date
field
folder
number
numeral
payee
"print" command
software
stub
word

OTHERS
by hand (adverbial)
check-writing (adj.)
open (adj.)

For Special Attention

- A **payee** is a person or company who is to receive the check.
- The **check stub** stays in the check folder or book to leave a record of the check.

By Hand

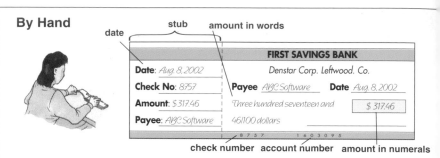

date   stub   amount in words

FIRST SAVINGS BANK

Date: *Aug. 8, 2002*   Denstar Corp. Leftwood. Co.
Check No: *8757*   Payee *ABC Software*   Date *Aug. 8, 2002*
Amount: *$317.46*   *Three hundred seventeen and*   *$ 317.46*
Payee: *ABC Software*   *46/100 dollars*

8 7 5 7   1 6 0 3 0 9 5

check number   account number   amount in numerals

Alice wrote out a check and filled out the stub.

She tore the check out of the folder.

Then her boss signed the check.

By Computer

Paymaster Financial Program

Alice opened her check-writing software.

checking
Date [Aug. 8, 2001]
Payee [ABC Software]
Amount [$317.46]
check No 8757

She entered the date, payee, and amount in the open fields.

PRINT

Then she clicked on the "print" command...

...and the check was printed out.

50 Sending Out a Bill

Key Vocabulary

VERBS
double-check
file
mail
prepare
print out
put [put]
review
send [sent] out
staple

NOUNS
amount
bill
copy
customer
file
invoice
item
price
purchase order

ADJECTIVES
due
total

For Special Attention

• To **double-check** something means to check or review it again.
• If a bill or invoice is **due**, it means it is time to be paid. If it is **overdue**, it means the payment is late.

Albert prepared an invoice for a customer.

He reviewed the items and prices on the purchase order...

...and double-checked the total amount due.

After he printed out three copies of the invoice,...

...he stapled one copy to the purchase order...

...and put it in the customer's file.

Then he filed one copy of the invoice.

He mailed the other copy of the invoice to the customer.

Key Vocabulary

VERBS
endorse
file
need
open
place
post
receive
record
review
stamp

NOUNS
accounts receivable
check
computer
customer
file
information
invoice
payment
safe

ADJECTIVE
paid

For Special Attention

- When you **record** or **post** something, you make a written note of it.
- An **accounts receivable file** lists the payments which are to be made to your company.
- When you **endorse** a check, you put your name or your company name on the back of the check. This is called your **endorsement.**

Time to enter this payment.

Alice needed to record a payment from a customer...

...so she opened the accounts receivable file on her computer.

After she reviewed the information on the check,...

...she endorsed it.

Then she posted the payment in the computer file...

...and stamped the invoice as paid.

She placed the check in a safe...

...and filed the invoice.

Key Vocabulary

VERBS
approve
attach
bring [brought]
count out
fill out
leave [left]
sign
tear [tore] out
unlock
work

NOUNS
amount
box
carbon copy
manager
petty cash
postage
receipt
reimbursement
strong box
voucher

ADJECTIVE
correct

For Special Attention

- **Petty cash** is an amount of money a business keeps available to pay small expenses.
- When an amount of money you have spent for something is returned to you, you are receiving **reimbursement.**
- A **voucher** is a kind of receipt that is given to show money has been paid.
- When you give your **approval,** it means you agree with something.

Albert brought a postage receipt to Alice for reimbursement.

> Hi, Alice. Could I get reimbursed for this postage?

Alice filled out a petty cash voucher...

...and her manager approved it.

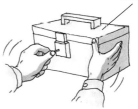

She unlocked the petty cash box...

strong box

> ...and that's 7.85.
> Thanks, Alice.

...and counted out the correct amount for Albert.

Albert signed the voucher.

Then Alice tore the voucher out, leaving a carbon copy behind.

She attached the voucher to the receipt.

53

Getting Supplies from a Stockroom

Key Vocabulary

VERBS
cross out
fill out
get [got]
leave [left]
note
notice
open
order
stack
take [took] out
unpack

NOUNS
amount
box
cabinet
computer disk
file folder
form
inventory sheet
package
paper
ream
stockroom
supplies
supply cabinet

OTHERS
last (adj.)
more (adv.)
neatly (adv.)
new (adj.)

For Special Attention

- A **stockroom** is a place where supplies are stored or kept. It is also called a **supply room.**
- **Inventory** refers to a list of all the items a company has available.
- A **requisition** is a request for something.
- A **ream** of paper is a pack of 500 sheets.

Matt opened the supply cabinet.

He took out two computer disks.

Then he crossed them out on the inventory sheet...

...and noted the new amount.

As he opened a box,...

Time to order more of these.

...he noticed there was only one file folder.

So he filled out a form to order more.

Before he left, he unpacked a box of paper...

...and stacked the reams neatly in the cabinet.

54 Dealing with Accidents

Key Vocabulary

VERBS
bandage
bring [brought]
call
clean
complete
cut [cut]
deal [dealt] with
fall [fell]
get [got] out
injure
move
stay

NOUNS
accident
accident report
back
break room
emergency
  number
first aid kit
hand
hospital
paramedics
wound

ADJECTIVES
minor
serious

For Special Attention

- A **serious** injury is more harmful than a **minor** injury. A serious injury usually requires medical attention while a minor injury usually doesn't.
- An **emergency number** is a telephone number you call when something has happened that needs attention quickly.
- A **wound** happens when the skin is damaged or cut.

A Serious Accident

Tina fell in the break room.

She injured her back and couldn't move.

Matt called the emergency number.

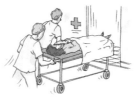

Then he stayed with Tina.

The paramedics brought Tina to the hospital,...

...and Matt completed an accident report.

A Minor Accident

Albert cut his hand...

...so he got out the first aid kit.

He cleaned the wound,...

...and he bandaged it.

Key Vocabulary

VERBS

arrive
blink
bring [brought]
call
change
close
discover
find [found]
fix
handle
leave [left]
mop up
notice
overflow
replace
see [saw]
vacuum up

NOUNS

air conditioning
break room
bulb
carpet
coffee maker
fan
janitor
light
light bulb
maintenance
night crew
note
office
pipe
plumber
problem
repair person
repair service
restroom
shut-off valve
sign
spill
thermostat
water
water pipe
work
worker

OTHERS

bad (adj.)
broken (adj.)
excess (adj.)
unusually (adv.)
warm (adj.)
warning (adj.)
wet (adj.)

A Bad Light Bulb

Hmmm. That bulb needs to be replaced.

Please replace bulb

The light in Alice's office was blinking,...

...so she left a note for the night crew.

A maintenance worker saw the note...

A Spill

What a mess!

The coffee maker overflowed in the break room.

...and changed the bad bulb.

Hi, Jim. This is Alice here. Could you send someone, please?

CAUTION WET FLOOR

Alice called maintenance.

A janitor mopped up the spill...

...and left a warning sign nearby.

For Special Attention

- **maintenance** = the act of taking care of something, or **maintaining** it.
- **Excess** means extra or more than enough.

A Broken Water Pipe

What happened here?

When Alice arrived at work, the carpet near her office was very wet.

So that's the problem.

She discovered a broken pipe in the restroom.

That will work for now.

She closed the water shut-off valve,...

Hello. We have a broken water pipe in our office.

...and called a plumber.

Good as new!

After the plumber fixed the pipe,...

...a worker vacuumed up the excess water from the carpet.

A Problem with the Air Conditioning

I don't think the air conditioning is working.

Albert noticed that the office was unusually warm.

We're having a problem with our air conditioning.

He called maintenance.

We'll have to call the heating and cooling company.

The maintenance worker found a problem with the thermostat.

Myers Heating and Cooling.

...and it looks like the thermostat is bad.

He called a repair service.

This should help a little bit for now.

Then he brought some fans to the office.

This feels much better.

Later, a repair person replaced the thermostat.

Key Vocabulary

VERBS

activate
ask
bring
  [brought]
close
deal [dealt]
  with
empty
escort
find [found]
get [got] rid of
go [went]
handle
have [had]
help
keep [kept]
leave [left]
lock
punch in
put [put]

remove
report
see [saw]
set [set]
shred
use
walk away

NOUNS

alarm
alarm code
building
computer
  monitor
desk
document
door
feeder
file cabinet
front door
guard
hallway
machine
man
office

paper
paper clip
person
precaution
purse
recycle bin
security
security
  screen
sheet
shredder
strip
visitor
workroom

ADJECTIVES

confidential
out of sight
ready
several
shredded
small
unfamiliar
unwanted

Setting an Alarm

Matt was ready to leave the office.

At the door, he punched in the alarm code.

After the alarm was activated,...

...Matt went out the door and closed it.

Then he locked the door.

Dealing with an Unwanted Visitor

I haven't seen him before.

Can I help you?

Sorry. I didn't hear what you said.

Albert saw an unfamiliar person in the hallway.

When Albert asked if he could help him,...

...the man walked away.

For Special Attention

- If something has been **activated**, it is ready to be used.
- If you **escort** someone, it means you go with him or her.
- When you **shred** something, you tear it into small pieces.

- **Precautions** are things done in order to keep something else from happening.
- Something that is **out of sight** is hidden from view. It can't be seen.

Albert reported him to security.

The guard found the man...

...and escorted him to the front door of the building.

Shredding Documents

Alice had some confidential documents to get rid of.

She brought the documents to the office workroom...

...and removed the paper clips.

feeder

Then she put several sheets in the shredder feeder.

The machine shredded the documents into small strips.

Alice emptied the shredded paper into the recycle bin.

Other Security Precautions

locking desks and file cabinets

keeping purses out of sight

using a security screen on a computer monitor

Appendix 1: American Measurements and Money

	American	Metric
Weight	1 pound [1 lb.] (16 ounces)	0.45 kilogram (kg)
	1 ounce [1 oz.]	28.35 grams (g)
Distance	1 mile [1 mi.] (5280 feet)	1.609 kilometers (km)
	1 yard [1 yd.] (3 feet)	0.914 meter (m)
	1 foot [1 ft.] (12 inches)	0.3048 meter (m)
	1 inch [1 in.]	2.54 centimeters (cm)
Volume/Capacity	1 gallon [1 gal.] (4 quarts)	3.785 liters (l)
	1 quart [1 qt.] (2 pints)	0.946 liter (l)
	1 pint [1 pt.] (2 cups)	0.473 liter (l)
	1 cup [1 c.] (8 fluid ounces)	236.6 milliliters (ml)
	1 fluid ounce [1 fl. oz.]	29.57 milliliters (ml)

Temperature

F = Fahrenheit   C = Celsius

212°F	100°C
90°F	32°C
75°F	24°C
50°F	10°C
32°F	0°C
0°F	-18°C

US Money

One dollar = 100 cents

Amount	Other names for it
1000 dollars	a grand
1 dollar	a buck
50 cents	a half dollar, half a buck
25 cents	a quarter
10 cents	a dime
5 cents	a nickel
1 cent	a penny

Appendix 2: Irregular Forms

Irregular Verbs

The following verbs from the text do not have the usual "-ed" past forms. Some of the verbs in the list below (e.g. *take*) occur in many different combinations (e.g. *take off*). In these combinations, the irregular past forms are the same as for the simple verb. For example, the past form of *take off* is *took off*.

Infinitive: Be

Present	Past	Past Participle
am	was	been
are	were	
is		

These forms also occur in *be going to* and *there+be*.

Infinitive: Have

Present	Past	Past Participle
have	had	had
has		

These forms also occur in *have to*.

Other Irregular Verbs

Infinitive	Past	Past Participle
begin	began	begun
bind	bound	bound
break down	broke down	broken down
bring	brought	brought
buy	bought	bought
choose	chose	chosen
come	came	come
deal with	dealt with	dealt with
do	did	done
drive	drove	driven
eat	ate	eaten
fall	fell	fallen
feed	fed	fed
find	found	found
forget	forgot	forgotten
get	got	gotten/got
give	gave	given
go	went	gone
hang	hung	hung
hear	heard	heard
hit	hit	hit
keep	kept	kept
leave	left	left
let	let	let

Infinitive	Past	Past Participle
make	made	made
pay	paid	paid
proofread	proofread	proofread
put	put	put
read	read	read
ring	rang	rung
run	ran	run
say	said	said
see	saw	seen
send	sent	sent
set up	set up	set up
shut	shut	shut
sit	sat	sat
slide	slid	slid
speak	spoke	spoken
spend	spent	spent
stick	stuck	stuck
take	took	taken
tear	tore	torn
tell	told	told
throw	threw	thrown
wake	woke	woken
wear	wore	worn
write	wrote	written

Process:

Key Vocabulary

Process:

Key Vocabulary

Process:

Key Vocabulary

To the Teacher

The English You Need for the Office (EYNO) uses pictures of common processes to help students develop a broad base of vocabulary useful in their jobs. Verbs receive special emphasis. Unlike other pictorial resources (such as picture dictionaries), *EYNO* goes beyond nouns to present a full range of essential vocabulary.

This material is ideal for mixed-level training situations. The pictures make it suitable for students at the beginning level, but the vocabulary will be of interest even to higher-level students, many of whom have never been taught such basic English in such great detail. The printed text and the pictures will acquaint students with the written forms of the vocabulary. A recording of this text is also available so students can learn the spoken forms of the vocabulary. A multi-skills activity book (including listening activities) is available separately and is accompanied by a separate recording.

Aims

A few of the aims central to *EYNO* are:
- to address vocabulary that is usable in a wide variety of office settings
- to activate readers' event schemata—their expectations about how ordinary office activities usually proceed
- to concentrate on the most essential and picturable steps in those activities
- to focus on verbs, since they are the key to accurate communications about events
- to create pictorial associations for key vocabulary

Organization

Each chapter focuses very narrowly on one process and depicts it in one or two pages. The chapters are grouped into eight larger sections, each of which could form a unit in a training course. Still, the chapters of *EYNO* are independent of one another. They do not have to be used sequentially. If your students have no need for a certain chapter, you can skip it without compromising their ability to understand later chapters. This gives course planners maximum flexibility in customizing a course to the needs of the students.

At the back of the book are several helpful resources, including appendices about U.S.-style measurements, U.S. currency, and irregular verbs. There are also pages titled "Processes: My Way," which may be photocopied. These can help students react individually to the material and recast it to fit their own circumstances. No book can account for all possible procedural variations from office to office. However, these pages give students an opportunity for showing—in writing, in pictures, or both—how things actually go at their own workplaces.

The index is very detailed and can be used to help students infer the features of a vocabulary item. For example, a student who encounters the verb "attach" on p. 51 (in connection with distributing mail) may want to use the index to find the other instances of "attach". By considering these all together, the student may develop a stronger sense of the item's meaning.

Conversational material arising out of each chapter is also provided at the back of the book (plus a recorded version). These will be useful to students to hear native speakers in natural office situations and to model similar conversations from their own experience.

We hope you and your students enjoy *EYNO* and the lively, action-based lessons that can be built from it.

Index

The terms indexed are all those appearing in captions, labels, and headings in the main text. Explanatory vocabulary from the "For Special Attention" sections is not indexed.

The index does not include:
- determiners (*a, the, any, each,* possessives, etc.)
- personal pronouns
- universal/partitive pronouns (*everyone, anyone, someone, something,* etc.)
- prepositions
- conjunctions
- proper names of characters (*Tina, Albert,* etc.)

Part–of–speech codes used in the index

n - noun	adj. - adjective
v - verb	adv. - adverb adv'l- adverbial

For ease of reference:
- common collocations (e.g., *say goodbye, by hand*) are listed as such
- some past participles of verbs (e.g., *broken, shredded*) are listed as adjectives
- some gerunds (e.g., *word-processing*) are listed as nouns
- a noun that must be plural in a given meaning is listed in the plural

Otherwise, terms are listed in their base forms — nouns in the singular, verbs in the infinitive, adjectives and adverbs in the positive.

Index

M

N

O

P

CONVERSATION PRACTICE MATERIAL CHAPTER BY CHAPTER

For each chapter the Conversation Practice follows the reading of the main text.

All characters are fictitious, so are all Internet addresses and (except as noted) the names of all products, companies, and groups portrayed in this work. Any resemblance to actual persons, products, or other entities is coincidental and unintended.

An asterisk * indicates that the word does not appear in the same chapter of the main text.

Chapter 1

Helen: Would you like some coffee with your breakfast?
Matt: I haven't got time for breakfast. It's 8:00.
Helen: Well, I've packed your lunch. It's in the bag.
Matt: Thanks, dear. I'll put it in my briefcase now.

Chapter 2

Matt: Alice, my door is open. I didn't unlock it. Did you?
Alice: No, Matt. Perhaps we should call security.
Matt: Yes, that's a good idea.
Alice: I can't see anything missing,* but I'll call the guard now.

Chapter 3

Matt: I need a new I.D. badge.
Tina: See the supervisor at security. He'll take your old one.
Matt: How will I get through the security desk?
Tina: They'll give you a temporary pass.

Chapter 4

Alice: This is the sign-in book, Sam. Every morning you have to write your name and the time in the book.
Sam: Thanks. At my last workplace* we had a punch-in system.
Alice: Oh, yes?
Sam: Yes, we had to punch our time card into a time clock.

Chapter 5

Matt: Good morning, Alice. I'll just put my lunch in the refrigerator.
Alice: Yes, we can then discuss the sales report.
Matt: Would you like a cup of coffee?
Alice: Thanks a lot.

Chapter 6

Matt: Alice, how many appointments have we got today?
Alice: Three. They're on your personal computer.
Matt: Oh, yes. I'll put them into my electronic organizer now.
Alice: And we have a meeting at 12:00 with Mr. Ferris.

Chapter 7

hˢ ¡ ᴛo This is our voice-mail system. When the message light blinks, you have a message.

Sam: Oh, yes. What do I do?

Alice: You press the message button, pick up the receiver and enter your PIN which is 583.

Sam: 583. I'll remember* that.

Chapter 8

Alice: This is our break room. Here's the coffee and there are some newspapers.

Sam: Where's Matt?

Alice: I think he's in the restroom.

Sam: I'll make the coffee for us. I brought in some cookies, too.

Chapter 9

Alice: Here's our cafeteria. You can get hot food from the steam table or a sandwich from the sandwich bar.

Sam: I feel like a salad.

Alice: The salad bar is over there and you pay the cashier over there.

Sam: Thanks very much, Alice.

Chapter 10

Matt: Are you going to the cafeteria, Tina?

Tina: No, I've got a bag lunch today.

Matt: What have you got?

Tina: A container of soup. I'm going to heat* it in the microwave.

Chapter 11

Alice: We're going out to a restaurant for lunch, Sam. Do you want to come?

Sam: No, thanks. I have to run some errands.

Alice: Where are you going?

Sam: I'm going to the post office to mail a package.

Chapter 12

Matt: Hello, Helen. I'll be working late today.

Helen: Oh, dear. When will you be home?

Matt: I have to file some documents and wait for* a courier.

Helen: Okay. I'll hold* dinner* for you.

Chapter 13

Alice: It's 5:00 now, Sam. You can sign out.

Sam: Oh, yes, so I write my name and time in the sign-in book again, do I?

Alice: Yes.

Sam: There we are.

Chapter 14

Matt: I'm doing a summary of the most recent sales figures, Alice.

Alice: Oh yes! Can I help?

Matt: The deadline is next Monday. Can you help with the print outs?

Alice: Okay, that's fine*.

Chapter 15

Alice: How is the summary going, Matt?
Matt: Well. I need more information on our sales of modem parts.
Alice: I can get that for you. Do you think we'll be finished on schedule?
Matt: Yes. No problem.

Chapter 16

Henry: Who's chairing the meeting this morning?
Alice: Tina. I hope it doesn't last long. Are there many items on the agenda?
Henry: Only three, but I think there are some new announcements.
Alice: Well, I have to leave at 11.00.

Chapter 17

Alice: I have an appointment* this afternoon, Sam. Would you be able to take the minutes for me?
Sam: I've never done it before. What do I do?
Alice: You have to write down the names of the people there, the time that the meeting starts and ends, read out the minutes of the last meeting and take notes of all important* things that are said.
Sam: I can do that.

Chapter 18

Alice: Would you take a look at this memo, please, Matt?
Matt: Certainly. Oh, it needs to go to Mr. Franks as well.
Alice: What shall I change?
Matt: Just change the copy list and make an extra copy for him.

Chapter 19

Alice: Can I borrow a self-adhesive notepad? I need to leave a note for Jane.
Matt: Sure.
Alice: What time is it?
Matt: 3:30.

Chapter 20

Jane: Can you help me set the photocopier?
Albert: Certainly. Put your original on the glass. How many copies do you want?
Jane: Twelve. But I need to enlarge them.
Albert: Press the number in here and the enlargement button here.

Chapter 21

Leo: I'm here to fix the copier.
Alice: Oh, yes. Over here.
Leo: What's the problem?
Alice: The paper keeps jamming in the rollers.

Chapter 22

Matt: Could you please collate and staple these copies for me, Alice?
Alice: O.K. What should I do with them when I've finished?
Matt: Give one copy to Hal, one copy to me and one for the file.
Alice: And I'll give the originals back to you.

Chapter 23

Alice: Matt wants us to punch and bind these ten copies of the report.
Sam: How does he want them bound?
Alice: We'll use this paper punch and put them in these 3-ring binders.
Sam: I can do that for you.

Chapter 24

Sam: Brian has asked me to file this letter* to Oxmoor Products in our customers file, but I can't find a file for Oxmoor.
Alice: Well, you'll have to start a new one, then.
Sam: How?
Alice: Type the name, Oxmoor Products, on a label and stick it on a folder. Then file the folder in the filing cabinet.

Chapter 25

Alice: What's in the mail this morning, Joe?
Joe: Quite a lot for your department. There're two confidential letters for Mr. Harden, some mail for Ms. Clark and lots of junk mail.
Alice: I always throw out the junk mail. What's the magazine?
Joe: 'Good Business'. That's always a good read.

Chapter 26

Matt: Are you sure this address is correct, Alice?
Alice: Yes, I think so. I'll just look on their letterhead.
Matt: I was sure their company was in Idaho not Iowa.
Alice: Ah, you're right. It's Idaho.

Chapter 27

Matt: Here's some mail that needs postage, Alice.
Alice: Three letters and a package. Do you want this letter to go by international airmail?
Matt: Yes, please.
Alice: I'll send them off today.

Chapter 28

Alice: I'd like to send this package by express delivery.
Brian: Sure! Just fill out this waybill.
Alice: How long will it take to get there?
Brian: You can have overnight or three-day service.

Chapter 29

Matt: Oh, good morning. My name is Matt, Account 7026459. I'm waiting for an express package from you. Can you tell me when I can expect it?
Connie: Do you have a tracking number, Sir?
Matt: Yes, it's XD 40598.
Connie: Ah, yes. It'll be arriving tomorrow at four o'clock.

Chapter 30

Alice: Good morning. I'm looking for a listing for The Twelve Bells restaurant* in Seattle.
Paul: Yes, that's 816-555-342.
Alice: 816-555-342. Thank you very much.
Paul: No problem, ma'am.

Chapter 31

Alice: Good morning. Accounting. This is Alice.
Sam: Hello, Alice. This is Sam. I'm trying to find Matt.
Alice: He's in Marketing on the third floor.*
Sam: Thanks, Alice. I'll go up there now.

Chapter 32

Helen: Good morning, Mr. Chu's office. Helen speaking.

Albert: Hi, Helen. It's Albert. Is Mr. Chu in?

Helen: No, he's not here at the moment. Can I take a message?

Albert: No, I'll call him back later. Thanks a lot.

Chapter 33

Ben: Good morning, this is Ben McCormack. Can I speak to Matt please?

Alice: He's in Accounting just now. Please hold and I'll transfer you.

Ben: Thanks a lot.

Alice: Any time, Mr McCormack.

Chapter 34

Betty: Good morning. This is Betty in Marketing.

Bob: This is Bob from Cain's Machinery. Can I speak to Matt, please?

Betty: He's at lunch at the moment. Can I take a message?

Bob: Yes. Could you ask him to call me at 555-983? Thanks.

Chapter 35

Matt: Can I speak to Helen, please?

Prue: I'm sorry, she's not in the office right now. Can I take a message?

Matt: Yes, please. This is Matt Johnson of Oxmoor. Could you ask her to call me before 5:00 at 555-277?

Prue: Certainly. I'll give her the message when she comes in.

Chapter 36

Alice: This is our fax machine, Sam.

Sam: Ah, yes.

Alice: First you have to prepare a cover sheet for your fax saying who you're sending it to, the date, your name, the number of pages and the subject. Here are the cover sheets.

Sam: Thanks, Alice.

Chapter 37

Sam: Here's a fax that just came in, but I can't read page 5.

Alice: Send them a fax back telling them and they'll resend it.

Sam: What do I do with it when I've got all the pages?

Alice: Staple the pages together and deliver them to the recipient.

Chapter 38

Sam: The fax machine's broken. Where's the user's manual?

Alice: It's in the cupboard, but what's wrong with it?

Sam: The paper keeps on jamming.

Alice: If you can't fix it, call the repair service.

Chapter 39

Alice: This is your computer, Sam. You have to step on the power strip beneath your desk to start the computer.

Sam: O.K., press the power strip.

Alice: O.K. Then press the on/off button on the CPU and turn on the monitor.

Sam: Yes, that's what I did in my other job.

Chapter 40

Alice: When you want to shut down the computer, remember to save the document you're working on.
Sam: I will.
Alice: Then choose 'shut down' option from the menu and click OK. Remember to turn off the monitor and press the power strip again.
Sam: Okay.

Chapter 41

Sam: How do you spell Mr. Rosemount? It's not in the spell checker on the computer.
Alice: Look in his file in the filing cabinet.
Sam: Ah, here it is. R-O-S-E-M-O-U-N-T.
Alice: Yes, I thought that's how it was spelled.

Chapter 42

Sam: The printer's not working.
Alice: Have you switched it on?
Sam: Yes, and I've previewed the document and set up the print job on the computer.
Alice: Check that there's paper in the feeder.

Chapter 43

Alice: When you want to receive your e-mails, you have to enter your password.
Sam: What's my password?
Alice: MARKB38. Once you type that in, you can see which e-mails you've received.
Sam: Thanks.

Chapter 44

Albert: There's always so much mail waiting for me when I come back.
Alice: I know. It makes you wonder whether it's worth going away on vacation.
Albert: And now I want to attach our monthly sales report to the e-mail and I can't find the file.
Alice: Hang on. I think I've got a copy on my computer. I'll copy it for you.

Chapter 45

Alice: Matt needs to travel* to South America next month. Can you go on line and find out the cheapest fares?
Sam: Sure.
Alice: Just go through a portal. We don't have a bookmark for a travel agent.*
Sam: Okay.

Chapter 46

Alice: I have to use the computer to type these labels. It's much better using the computer.
Sam: Yes, I don't know how we managed* without computers.
Alice: They're so much better for doing letters. You can make changes so easily.
Sam: And you can see how your document will look before you print it.

Chapter 47

Albert: Alice, I'm just totaling the receipts for last week and I noticed this one.
Alice: Yes, Albert. I did that one.
Albert: I think it's wrong. I think this was special* paper costing $15 a ream.*
Alice: Oh, yes. I think you're right. Sorry about that.

Chapter 48

Matt: I ordered some more stationery* last week and it's just arrived.
Alice: Is there an invoice with the delivery?
Matt: Yes.
Alice: I'll just make sure that every item on the invoice has been delivered and I'll issue a check for the invoice amount.

Chapter 49

Alice: Here's the check for Big Al's Stationery. Could you sign it for me, please?
Matt: Sure. Are they going to collect it or should it be mailed?
Alice: The vendor's stopping round this afternoon so I'll give it to him then.
Matt: Good.

Chapter 50

Albert: Alice, I was just filing an invoice in the customer file and I found this invoice that hasn't been paid yet.
Alice: Oh, dear. Yes, it looks like the customer hasn't paid us yet.
Albert: Could you send out a copy of this invoice and ask them to pay us within seven days?
Alice: Sure. I'll do that now.

Chapter 51

Alice: When we receive checks, you have to post the payment in the computer file, endorse the check and stamp the invoice as paid.
Sam: Where do I put the check?
Alice: In the safe. And file the invoice.
Sam: Okay.

Chapter 52

Albert: I've just bought some pens for the office.
Alice: Do you have a receipt?
Albert: Yes. They cost $4.95.
Alice: Okay. Here's the money. Sign this voucher, please.

Chapter 53

Matt: Oh, Alice. This is the last ream of paper for the photocopier. Can you order some more?
Alice: Sure, Matt. Do we need anything else?
Matt: You could check the floppy disks and the pens.
Alice: Right. I'll do that.

Chapter 54

Sam: Ow, I've sprained* my ankle.*
Alice: Don't walk on it. Sit down. I'll go and get the first-aid kit.
Sam: Thanks.
Alice: This bandage should help you.

Chapter 55

Sam: It's awfully hot in here.
Alice: I don't think the air conditioning is working properly.
Sam: Should I call the repair service?
Alice: Not yet. We'll call maintenance first.

Chapter 56

Alice: Sam, we have to shred some confidential documents today.

Sam: Okay. Where are we going?

Alice: The office workroom. You take the paper clips and staples out of them and I'll shred them.

Sam: And we'll put them in the recycle bin afterwards?

Alice: Yes.